Michael F-ing Bay

The Unheralded Genius in Michael Bay's Films

By
The Bitter Script Reader

Cover illustration by Keith Richner

Text Copyright © 2014 The Bitter Script Reader

All Rights Reserved

Table of Contents

Introduction	5
Transformers: Age of Extinction (2014)	13
Bad Boys (1995)	25
The Rock (1996)	38
Armageddon (1998)	53
Pearl Harbor (2001)	70
Bad Boys II (2003)	90
The Island (2005)	101
Transformers (2007)	116
Transformers: Revenge of the Fallen (2009)	132
Transformers: Dark of the Moon (2011)	144
Pain & Gain (2013)	158
Final Thoughts	172
Michael Bay Filmography	176
Acknowledgements	179
About the Author	181
Source Notes	182

4

Introduction

Suppose you were hosting a dinner party and invited the six most successful directors of all time, using the metric of domestic box office returns to determine the invite list. For as much as people claim that the Academy Awards only recognize smaller artier projects and shun mainstream movies, it might surprise you to realize that five of those six most successful filmmakers have not only been nominated, but also won Oscars in the Best Directing category.

Glancing over that list, you would find Steven Spielberg in first place with $4.15 billion in accumulated domestic box office, Robert Zemeckis in third with $2.1 billion, James Cameron in fourth at $1.97 billion, Peter Jackson in fifth at $1.88 billion, and Ron Howard in sixth with $1.83 billion. Yes, that indeed means the second most successful director of all time, a man who has earned $2.14 billion at the domestic box office, is the only one of these men to not be honored by the Academy Awards.

Who's that poor bastard who would have to sit awkwardly as the makers of *Titanic*, *Forrest Gump* and *A Beautiful Mind* swap stories about how to keep their Oscars golden? None other than Michael Bay.

Even if we were to change our criteria to be worldwide box office instead of domestic, Bay would still be left out. In that case, four of the top six most successful directors have won Oscars. Bay falls to number 3 here with $5.75 billion, right behind Spielberg's $9 billion and James Cameron's $6.13 billion. After that comes Peter Jackson with $5.56 billion in fourth; a win-less, nomination-less David Yates in fifth with $4.17 billion, and Zemeckis in sixth with $4 billion.

Seeing these correlations, one might conclude that perhaps filmmakers with mass appeal have been recognized for that particular sort of artistic brilliance. After all, it is no mere fluke that these directors have found their films to be consistently popular. Reaching a mass audience time and again isn't easy and certainly requires its own level of brilliance. Therefore, it's not hugely inexplicable that the Academy of Motion Picture Arts & Sciences would honor the most successful of those men not just with wins, but with multiple nominations.

Except for Michael Bay, the perpetual underdog.

Michael Bay is not a filmmaker who gets an abundance of respect from critics either. One need only to glance back nearly twenty years to the reviews of his first film *Bad Boys* to appreciate that. It is an interesting irony in that many of that film's reviews available via Rotten Tomatoes tend to focus largely on then-uber-producers Don Simpson and Jerry Bruckheimer as the architects of this cinematic mayhem. The director himself is mostly an afterthought. Yet today, after eleven films and over $5.75 billion in unadjusted worldwide gross, it's impossible to deny that this former music video director has left his mark on film history permanently.

Even so, it feels like Bay will forever be seeking respect, dismissed as a man who makes only mindless movies whose merits are limited to quick cuts and explosions.

For a long time I accepted that as the narrative on Michael Bay. His style of filmmaking certainly invites an emphasis on the superficial. To seek greater depth in one of his productions would initially appear to be as fruitless as obtaining celery at a candy story. But is the greater failing our own for being blinded by the eye candy? If a critique of Mr. Bay's work begins with the assumption that it's artless garbage, can it be a fair critique at all?

Artists become artists because they have something to say. We cannot hold them responsible for our own failing to listen.

A recent documentary called *Room 237* focused on several incredibly devoted fans of filmmaker Stanley Kubrick and their assumptions of his intentions when he made *The Shining*. It's a fascinating documentary not necessarily for what it can prove about Mr. Kubrick, but for what it reveals about the human capacity to find meaning in a work of art. Many of those featured in the documentary have theories that are incompatible with each other, and indeed, it becomes increasingly far-fetched to accept that Kubrick intended many of the more elaborate readings of the film that his faithful have found.

And yet those interpretations are there.

The fact we have not found anything of deeper artistry in Michael Bay's work does not mean there is nothing to find. It simply means that we have not looked hard enough.

These revelations came to me as I attempted to sort out my thoughts over Bay's latest film, *Transformers: Age of Extinction*. Though the film was commercially successful, (earning $100 million in its first weekend of domestic release alone) critics were not kind, scoring it a mere 17% on Rotten Tomatoes. The so-called "Top Critics" were even more united in their distaste for the film, as it only rated 5% among that demographic.

"Seemingly written by a thirteen-year old boy and directed by his walking erection, this one is nothing but a booming pile of rubble." – Neil Miller, *Film School Rejects*.

"The cinematic equivalent of being repeatedly hit over the head with a food mixer." - Alan Jones, *RadioTimes*.

"Even the diehard Transformers fans will be hard pressed not to admit that this movie stinks." – Lori Hoffman, *Atlantic City Weekly*.

Sometimes, we find what we expect to see in a film. Here, it's possible the critics' readings of the film is somewhat informed by their earlier experiences in the franchise. While seeking a fresh perspective, I did my best to accept the film on its own terms.

The more I thought about the film, the more I found it stimulating my thoughts. What if Bay was trying to slip in some subversive messages? What if all of us missed this because we had written him off long ago? Are we all like a primary school teacher who can't believe the class clown has turned in an A+ paper?

My theories formed the basis for my review of *Transformers: Age of Extinction*, posted to my blog "The Bitter Script Reader" on the Monday following that film's release. It quickly attracted notice on the net and at present is my third most-popular post of all time.

Perhaps I should back up and introduce myself. I came to Hollywood over a decade ago to become a screenwriter and like many aspiring writers, I soon found myself working in development. During my time in the business, I was a development assistant and script reader for a number of companies over the years, including some very successful production companies and one of the "big five" agencies. After several years in those positions, having read literally thousands of scripts, I grew weary of seeing the same mistakes over and over again. It felt like there should be a way to reach out to aspiring writers and let them know that what they think is original writing might be one of the clichés I saw six times a week.

In recent years, I had seen a number of writers use the internet to connect with their fanbase. Today, of course, via Twitter nearly every major writer has a following and is accessible for questions. Young people are gaining for free what it used to take years of experience in the industry to learn. Honestly, I envy this generation. When I was a teenager there were few industry professionals online in a public way. The most prominent was writer Ronald D. Moore, then of *Star Trek: Deep Space Nine*. Moore regularly interacted with Trek fans via the AOL boards and often answered questions about TV writing and the genesis of particular episodes. I learned probably as much about TV writing from him as I did in four years of school. This made me aware of the value in a website focused on writing. And so one day in early 2009, I launched my blog, offering my insight about screenwriting from the perspective of the reader who is usually the first person a script needs to get past.

My work history as a reader gave me a legitimate perspective and an authority on the subject. As the site evolved, I moved from merely documenting clichés of bad scripts to explaining why other stories worked so well. I like to think I removed some mystery from the screenwriting process and helped a number of aspiring writers to not get taken in by scams. There are so many books and services out there that seemed designed to just suck the money from gullible young writers looking for a quick short-cut. If giving away my advice for free hurt their business model, then I'm proud of that. I have a decent audience that comes back day-after-day and I just recently reached the milestone of 25,000 Twitter followers and growing.

More than five years after its creation, my blog stands as one of the most recognized and most respected sites about screenwriting. I've made a great many professional friends and industry contacts through my blog and my Twitter. It's opened a number of doors for me and given me a wonderful audience. For a long time, I had considered launching an e-book. An obvious idea would have been to compile a number of my blog posts into a book, but I doubted I could get many people to purchase what they could easily find for free in blog form. I also considered publishing transcripts of all my interviews with writers and other pros, but discarded that notion for much the same reason.

Eventually, it was clear I would need to produce original material for any book release. During my struggle to develop content that hadn't already been produced for the blog that I saw the latest *Transformers* film. Writing that review left me with so much to say not just about the film, but about Michael Bay, that I realized his entire catalog merited re-examination.

And thus was born the book you now hold in your hands, an intellectual journey into the world of Michael Bay. Though the *Age of Extinction* review is available on my blog, all other content is new to this release. Because of its role in sparking this examination of Bay's oeuvre, I have decided to begin the book with that review, and then flash back to the start of Bay's career, examining each feature film in chronological order. As you will see, *Age of Extinction* is the Rosetta Stone to Bay's themes and semiotics. Understanding that film can help unlock unnoticed themes in his earlier works. It is the final puzzle piece which illuminates that all of the other films were indeed intended to play on multiple levels. Were it not for the epiphanies *Age of Extinction* provoked, it is likely I would have remained blissfully ignorant of the subtleties contained within the rest of Bay's filmography.

I hope that this book encourages many of you to examine Bay's films and films beyond Bay's work with fresh eyes. We cannot always discover what we are not actively looking for. I spent nearly 20 years blind to some of the most exemplary and subtle genius in Mr. Bay's output because I came to it with an inflexible mind. For the sake of this examination, forget everything you knew or believed about Michael Bay and begin each movie from the standpoint that there is rarely a choice Bay makes without a higher purpose. When you give artists the benefit of the doubt, you may find them capable of the most extraordinary of feats.

And who knows? Perhaps one day, Bay won't be the one director awkwardly silent at the aforementioned dinner party once the topic turns to what makes a good Oscar acceptance speech.

Transformers: Age of Extinction (2014)

Release date: June 27, 2014
Written by Ehren Kruger
Produced by Don Murphy, Tom DeSanto, Lorenzo di Bonaventura
Budget: $210 million
Domestic box office: $244.4 million
Global box office: $1.03 billion

Transformers: Age of Extinction might be the most cinematically daring film of this decade, if not this century. It's a genuinely rare pleasure to be cognizant of film history being made as you watch celluloid (figuratively) unspool before you, but Michael Bay has never been a conventional filmmaker. With *Age of Extinction*, this Picasso of Pyro has produced a potent film as subversive and singular as anything one might find from John Waters or Michael Haneke.

"It would be nice to not have to do effects and big car crashes. I'm waiting for the great written word."

This is a quote from an interview Michael Bay gave fifteen years ago to *The Wesleyan Argus*, the school paper of his alma mater, Wesleyan University. By then, he was already famous for *Bad Boys, The Rock*, numerous music videos and was on the cusp of *Armageddon*'s release. At that point, it's probably not out of line to say that many dismissed him as a surface-level filmmaker. The irony of that attack is that charge is only plausible if those who subscribe to it limit their gaze to the flashy exterior that coats Bay's films like glaze on a donut, or baby oil on a desirable woman.

Much like The Beatles, whose pop exterior was merely the delivery method through which more complex and profound ideas were smuggled, Bay has always planted deeper themes for those willing to look for them. Anyone who appreciated his masterful reworking of the *Beauty & The Beast* tale in music video form could understand this. For those who don't know, the video for "I Would Do Anything For Love (But I Won't Do That)" tells the story of a singularly-beautiful creature who wins the love of desire incarnate... at the price of trading in his unique appearance for the grotesque visage of Meat Loaf.

Alas, Bay's work more often was appreciated (and derided) for its facile charms by those not in on the joke. Accordingly, Bay exaggerated their scale with each subsequent film, possibly in the futile hope that taking the material increasingly over-the-top would expose it as satire and criticism of the values so many erroneously assume those works endorse. And still the call went unheeded. It's impossible to think of any peer in his field who has been so aggressively deconstructive of his own work within the films he has helmed.

It was during this film that clarity finally dawned on me - Michael Bay is Daniel Clamp, the billionaire developer played with aplomb by John Glover in *Gremlins 2: The New Batch*. In that film, Clamp was responsible not only for a pending modernized redevelopment of Chinatown, but also a fully automated building that was quite often a source of consternation for those using it. It also proved to be the perfect romping ground for the Gremlins to destroy. Having survived that chaos, at the end of the film Clamp looks at his achievement with new eyes, saying, "Maybe it wasn't a place for people anyway. It was a place for things. You make a place for things... things come."

At some point, Michael Bay looked at the summer movies that arrived in the wake of his films, and realized he had turned summer into a place for things. *Armageddon* and *Pearl Harbor* are the sound and fury that made films like *G.I. Joe, Battleship* and *White House Down* possible. With *Age of Extinction*, Bay has finally reached the point where he's stopped being subtle about trying to implode the automated building he forged.

The summer's most meta line of dialogue is uttered by Kelsey Grammer's character, the true hero of the film, as he states, "A new era has begun. The age of Transformers is over..."

Taken together, the *Transformers* Tetralogy is the most intensely self-aware criticism of the MTV-style, explosion-happy, titillation-soaked style of filmmaking. For the last several *Transformers* films, Bay sought to make this motivation more obvious by recruiting Ehren Kruger for screenplay duties. One of the leading voices in film, Kruger is clearly of a like mind when it comes to making audiences confront the superficial nature of the works they submit their intelligence to.

Artists and critics often talk about "emotional truth" versus "logical truth." This is the justification by which a film doesn't have to make logical sense - or even adhere to its own stated logic - so long as it *feels* right. Does it makes sense, or is it even historically accurate, when President Roosevelt defies the odds to rise out of his wheelchair in *Pearl Harbor*? Absolutely not. But it provokes that sort of "never give up spirit" that is essential to the film. The genius of Kruger is that he carries this further.

Consider the ending of *Arlington Road*, where Jeff Bridges is played for a fool by terrorists who manipulate circumstances with god-like precision. . No less than the great Roger Ebert once misread this film, first tearing into the ending's plausibility issues, saying "The climax is so implausible we stop caring and start scratching our heads." He goes on to point out all the ways in which the bad guys plan doesn't make sense because it seemingly depends on factors impossible to foresee, asking, "How can anyone, even skilled conspirators, predict with perfect accuracy the outcome of a car crash? How can they know in advance that a man will go to a certain pay phone at a certain time, so that he can see a particular truck he needs to see?."

With respect to Mr. Ebert, this is the entire point. Kruger wasn't attempting to write a brilliant thriller, he was writing a brilliant criticism of brainless thrillers and attempting to provoke the audience into recognizing the smoke and mirrors behind them. For a film to tell you that its climactic twist was ironic or impressive should not be enough. "It doesn't make sense!" the film screams.

"And you lemmings lap it up every time!" When that moral failed to land, Kruger repeated the trick with *The Ring* - a film that ends with a moment that feels shocking and dangerous ("You didn't let her out, did you?") before reminding us that freeing Samara doesn't make things worse. She still is limited to only killing those who have watched her cursed tape.

Thus, it's impossible not to interpret *Age of Extinction* as two brilliant deconstructionists jam-banding on an action movie specifically designed to burn the house down. This is Kruger and Bay as Bialystock and Bloom, dropping "Springtime for Hitler" on an unsuspecting crowd like it's an atom bomb. (Appropriately, the soundtrack of the damned can only be provided by Imagine Dragons.)

With the fourth *Transformers*, Michael Bay finally accomplishes what the three previous films slowly laid the groundwork for - turning the Transformers into bad guys and the enemies of all mankind. The first film is idealistic and Spielberg-like for the first hour. It's the story of a teenage boy advancing into manhood by pursuing the desirable girl. It's a story as old as time and one gets the sense that were there no killer robots, Sam might win Mikaela's heart easily. But then the killer robots smash into Sam's narrative and from then on, the simple joys of independence from one's parents and pleasures of the flesh are cast aside.

Mayhem reigns and eventually casts a swath of destruction through Sam's life across two sequels. It's no accident that the romance Sam sought in the first film is destroyed by the time the third one comes around. We should not want these *Transformers*, Bay is telling us. We should not want these films. This prompted his most audacious move in the third film, replacing Megan Fox with a lingerie model. Bay must have wondered what more he had to do to let the audience know he was in on the joke. It was a decision that should have provoked outrage, followed by the realization that the action genre is so superficial that it simply doesn't matter who runs around screaming "Optimus!" Alas, the film was successful enough that Bay's clever intentions seem to have been lost.

Accordingly, that has led Bay and Kruger to up the ante in this latest outing. The theme of the Transformers being destructive to mankind has been taken from subtext to text. Even the ostensible "good guys," the Autobots are not heroes. They despise mankind and are currently hunted by them. Optimus Prime's first speech in the film is a violent threat directed at all humans. He's flabbergasted that humans would "betray" them after all they've done.

And what have the Autobots done except bring an interstellar war to the doorstep of a race that has no stakes in the battle? What has mankind done except have the audacity to build cities where the "good" and "bad" robots alike do immense battle without any concern for collateral damage? Optimus Prime is the herald for Armageddon and he and his disciples regard mankind as ungrateful because the Transformers haven't been greeted as liberators for a conflict for which they are completely responsible. Sure, they always justify it as trying to stop a hidden weapon or to vanquish a greater evil, but at the end of the day it remains their fight and their fight alone.

And that's when it hits you - *Transformers: Age of Extinction* is all about the Iraq War.

It is as pointed and liberal a criticism of neoconservative policy as you will find in a modern action film. Suddenly it no longer seems quite so inexplicable that this is the first *Transformers* film to not feature extensive cooperation from the U.S. military.

The subtext of the film is clear - Transformers are evil. Thus, *Transformers* movies are also evil and destructive to film. The Earth depicted in this series of films is justified in wanting all Transformers, good and bad, vanquished forever. The same goes for the soulless films that bring their exploits to the screen. Michael Bay must have smiled as he concocted this plot with his screenwriter, certain that if making Optimus Prime the villain wouldn't at last destroy this franchise and set him free, taking on a hot button topic like the Iraq War would.

Let's not mistake that criticism for anti-American sentiment, because Bay's other masterstroke is that the real hero of this film is a true patriot through and through. Kelsey Grammer plays a CIA agent who's made a secret pact with one faction of Transformers. With this, he gets their cooperation in hunting down all remaining Transformers - Autobot and Decepticon alike - and then mining them for spare parts to build machines that mankind will control themselves. Clearly Grammer's character has more common sense than any human featured in these films yet.

It's here that Bay and Kruger again confront the audience with the superficial filmic conventions they are used to embracing. In any other film, Grammer's character would be a sinister bad guy, someone whose death we cheer. Instead, time and again, he's the only character with any sense at all. He's mobilized a task force to hunt a dangerous insurgent (Optimus Prime) and was savvy enough to make this other race of Transformers realize the partnership benefits both of them. He's hunting Optimus Prime because he knows that the longer he's out there, the worse it will be for national security, heck, even global security.

The movie proves him right. From the time Optimus is turned back on, all he does is cause carnage and destruction while he and his cohorts regroup to be more effective at said destruction. Two entire cities are lain to waste needlessly, a point driven home at the end of the film. One might try to justify all of the devastation as the work of the bad guys coming after Optimus, but the movie's final shot makes it clear that Optimus could have flown off of the planet unaided at any time he wanted. Everything terrible that happens in this film is on Optimus Prime's shoulders.

Doubters of this theory might retort, "But if he's the hero, how does one rationalize him seemingly selling out for a stake in the company owned by Stanley Tucci's billionaire character?" Is it "selling out" to earn a living by utilizing your assets in return for compensation? Grammer's character Attinger is a sly meta-commentary on the parade of classy actors (John Malkovich, Jon Voight, Frances McDormand, and Tucci and Grammer themselves for that matter) often mocked and derided for appearing in films like this. Attinger has devoted his life to his country. His passion is patriotism, but that unfortunately doesn't pay the bills. It's no different for actors who are artistically fulfilled by the rich independent films that pay little. No one in Hollywood would begrudge any of those fine performers the compensation of a paycheck role, and thus, Attinger's "paycheck role" should not be treated as an indictment against him. We do not judge Grammer and Tucci for lending gravitas to this film for a fair price, nor do we condemn Attinger for his deal with Tucci's billionaire character.

It's telling that when Grammer's character dies, it's not in a confrontation with a human protagonist, such as the one played by Mark Wahlberg. His end comes from a cold-blooded shot by Optimus Prime. Tucked amid the total destruction of Hong Kong, it could have been a tiny act of violence, but the human scale of the brutality here at last brings into focus what a monster Optimus Prime is, acting above the law and summarily executing a man whose only true crime was trying to protect his nation from a proven threat.

Optimus Prime is a false god, unworthy of being cheered as a liberator or worshiped via the ubiquitous toys found in every store. This is a film designed to make every patriotic American want to burn their Optimus Prime toys in solidarity, then buy more to burn them again. For a while, it seemed that Bay was content just to destroy the genre of superficial blockbusters, but three movies clearly taught him that the merchandising will keep this series going forever. How does one defeat that?

By destroying the symbol that fuels the legend.

What Bay and Kruger do here, they do for the good of future generations of film. Alan Moore in his prime could not have achieved such a pointed deconstruction of the toy-to-movie form of entertainment.

The treatment of women is different this time out too. One of the most uncomfortably leering scenes in a PG-13 film was the "check under the hood" scene in the first *Transformers* where the camera ogled Megan Fox with such force it's a wonder her clothes didn't melt. Her entrance bending over a motorcycle in the second film was perhaps even more exploitative, and in the third chapter, her Victoria's Secret replacement fared little better.

By comparison *Age of Extinction's* Nicola Peltz is practically covered in a burka. There are no bare midriffs, barely any cleavage, no bending-over shots and perhaps only a fleeting moment or two where Bay's camera admires her from behind. Moreover, she's time and again pretty much the only character with any real common sense. Her father, Cade, likes to think he's laying down the law, but for the all the overprotective vibes he puts out, it's pretty obvious if he was left without her, he'd starve within a week. Cade makes such terrible decisions from his first moment on screen that the movie seems to be testing how far it can push it before the audience realizes their sexist impulses and star worship have led them to embrace the wrong character as the "hero."

The story between Cade and his daughter can't help but stir memories of *Armageddon*. The girl has been secretly dating an older guy against her father's "no boys" rule. It starts off seeming like a replay of Bruce Willis's Harry Stamper and his rage at finding out one of his workers (Ben Affleck) is dating his daughter (Liv Tyler.) By the end of the film, Harry sacrifices himself so that Affleck's character can live and look after his girl.

Towards the end of *Age of Extinction*, Bay gives us a moment designed to evoke that same passing of the baton, with Cade diving back into battle after telling his girl he loves her and telling her boyfriend to take care of her. The boyfriend (the wussiest alpha male ever to wander into a Bay film) raises no objection. But Peltz's character doesn't take this shit. She immediately tells her boyfriend and Bumblebee that they're going back for Cade. Much is made of this, for when Bumblebee returns to battle, Optimus Prime shouts "I gave you an order!"

Not only does Wahlberg's lunkhead Cade not have to sacrifice himself, but he's saved entirely by the only person who's given good advice the entire film, his daughter. The connection couldn't be clearer. Peltz is essentially Penny and Wahlberg is Inspector Gadget, the hapless fool who thinks he knows what he's doing while the person he's technically responsible for is the one who really knows the score.

Who knew Michael Bay was a feminist? Until viewing this film, I admit it never occurred to me. (Or maybe he just likes *Inspector Gadget*.)

To return to the film as a whole, the excess isn't cranked to 11 here, it's spun all the way up to 22. *Of course* the movie verges on three hours – it's *supposed* to be a relentless assault on our senses. The only way the comparison between this film and Alex DeLarge's reconditioning in *A Clockwork Orange* could be more pointed was if the Imagine Dragons soundtrack included Beethoven's "Ode to Joy." Bay stuffs us full of pixels and pyrotechnics like a disciplinarian father forcing his son to smoke an entire carton of cigarettes after catching him smoking.

Transformers: Age of Extinction is anarchist filmmaking at its finest and the most subversive studio film released in decades. Every moment necessary, each scene part of a rich tapestry that film scholars will be analyzing and debating for centuries. I give this film four thumbs up, because in true Bay-like excess, why only give two thumbs when you can give four?

Bad Boys (1995)

Release date: April 7, 1995
Story by George Gallo
Screenplay by Michael Barrie & Jim Mulholland and Doug Richardson
Produced by Don Simpson, Jerry Bruckheimer
Budget: $19 million
Domestic box office: $65.8 million
Global box office: $141.4 million

Bad Boys and its sequel are unique among the films we will discuss in this book because they are the only two films in the Bay filmography that I had not previously seen until I embarked on this project. The benefit to this is that I was in a position to examine Michael Bay's earliest work with virgin eyes, though that also means I lack the context of someone who experienced the film upon its release. In the case of this film, that makes a rather significant difference.

Bad Boys is perhaps the most un-Michael Bay movie that Michael Bay has ever directed. It's fascinating to examine it after ten subsequent films have cemented the idea of what a Bay film should look and feel like. Though there are explosions, gun play and a few isolated examples of the trademark Bay-spin camera move, it lacks the Bay color palate, the oiled-up curvy women, and the fast cuts reminiscent of commercials or MTV videos. Many of you perhaps appreciate this warning and will take it as motivation to stay away, I will note that this film isn't above getting Will Smith shirtless, making it practically a "chick-flick" by what most consider "Bay standards."

It's a contrast to the early works of other directors who have a signature style. Quentin Tarantino's first film was *Reservoir Dogs*, which displays much of his trademark wit and character-driven dialogue. The Tarantino violence, which is alternately laced with humor and brutality also emerges fully formed, as does his use of older music cues. True, Tarantino had honed his voice as a writer before stepping behind the camera here, but the fact remains, *Reservoir Dogs* is "a Tarantino film." ('70s music cues and exploitation riffs for everyone!)

It's a pattern to be found with most filmmakers who have distinctive styles. Often they launch their careers with a low-budget film. In this way, the fact that the film requires less money and fewer investors allows the director to retain more control over the final product. There's also an argument to be made that such limitations force greater creativity in the script. A few examples of such directors include Darren Aronofsky (*Pi*), Kevin Smith (*Clerks*), M. Night Shyamalan (*Praying With Anger*), or to reach back even further, George Lucas (*THX-1138*).

Bad Boys is not a film on that level in either an artistic sense or a budgetary sense. Some of this is due to the fact that Bay is not a writer and it was not his creative impulse that drove this project. He was – in the vernacular of Hollywood – a "shooter." This is a term applied to directors who are more valued for their technical competence and workman-like ethic than any deeper artistic sensibilities they bring to the work.

Prior to this film, Michael Bay had directed a number of music videos and commercials. His visual flair made him an attractive candidate for this action film, but when producers hire a man like Bay, they're more concerned with having a director who will get the coverage they need, make their days, and stay on schedule. This is particularly true of *these* producers, Don Simpson and Jerry Bruckheimer, a team that were among the most successful of the previous decade. *Bad Boys* was always destined to be seen as part of their legacy.

As *Entertainment Weekly's* Owen Gleiberman wrote in his review of *Bad Boys*, "Beginning with that porno-aerobic synth-pop daydream *Flashdance* (always one of my guilty pleasures), and continuing on through *Beverly Hills Cop*, *Top Gun*, and *Days of Thunder*, Simpson and Bruckheimer created an aesthetic that delivered the adrenaline thrust of a cocaine high. Their movies were rushes - slickly galvanic fantasies." It's hard to remember, but at the time, this film was seen much more in context of those past glories of the producers and not the inception of a career that would become one of Hollywood's most successful. Fittingly, even today, Bad Boys plays far more like a Simpson/Bruckheimer film than a Bay one.

The Simpson-Bruckheimer saga is worthy of its own book, and in such a book, *Bad Boys* would only occupy one of the waning chapters, akin to *Topaz*'s placement in an Alfred Hitchcock retrospective. *Bad Boys* might not feel much like a Michael Bay movie, but it is absolutely a Simpson-Bruckheimer joint. It most resembles the two *Beverly Hills Cop* films the pair produced, to the point where a viewer new to all of those films might not realize that *Bad Boys* came a full eight years after *Beverly Hills Cop II*. In terms of tone, style and humor, the two films are close cousins to each other.

Don Simpson was the party animal of the two, the wild man to Jerry Bruckheimer's more conservative style. The stories about Simpson were already legend in his own time and has been chronicled in numerous books, including *High Concept: Don Simpson and the Culture of Hollywood Excess* by Charles Fleming. For the purposes of this examination, the most important fact to realize is that Simpson would only produce two further films after *Bad Boys*: *Dangerous Minds* and *The Rock*. He died of a drug-related heart failure on January 19, 1996. Though *Bad Boys* would prove to launch the second act for the Simpson-Bruckheimer team, Don Simpson took his curtain call early.

I recap all of this in part to set-up the fact that on this film Michael Bay was the hired gun and his producers were the 800-pound gorillas. Thus, Bay had little expectation of his artistic sensibilities overriding those of his producers. This was their movie, not his.

In its early conceptions, the two lead roles were not to be played by Will Smith and Martin Lawrence, but rather Dana Carvey and Jon Lovitz, a detail reported by numerous sources at the time, including *The New York Times*. The initial casting suggests a more heavily comedic tone for the film, though one has to remember that in 1995, Will Smith was still the star of *The Fresh Prince of Bel-Air* and not one of the biggest global superstars while Martin Lawrence's popularity was also cresting due to his sitcom *Martin*. Both versions of the film would have been an action comedy with sitcom stars. The difference is that the version that was made probably had a little more edge and sex appeal to it. I suppose it was a loss to all of us that we were denied the raw sensual pleasure of seeing Jon Lovitz chase after a perp with his shirt open.

    The story centers on two cops who have three days to recover 100 pounds of drugs stolen right out of police custody. That earlier bust was what made Smith and Lawrence's characters' (Mike Lowrey and Marcus Burnett, respectively) careers and with it looking like an inside job, the DEA is going to take over the case in a matter of days. One of Lowrey's informants, a woman named Max, is killed by the drug kingpin who stole the heroin. A friend of Max's named Julie, played by Tea Leoni witnesses the murder and flees to find the cop that Max said she always trusted, Mike Lowrey. This is complicated when Lowrey is unavailable and so Burnett steps in, pretending to be his partner. A good chunk of the story after than is spent with happily-married Marcus trying to pass himself off as well-off bachelor Lowrey to Julie.

    In all frankness, the mistaken-identity farce doesn't really work. Bay doesn't quite have the handle on the tone to allow the joke to sustain for the length the film prolongs it. A more comically-deft hand might have salvaged this, but it's also hard to imagine a Simpson-Bruckheimer film becoming that overtly funny. There's also the fact that this comedic subplot doesn't allow the humor to integrate into the main plot as effortlessly as Eddie Murphy's antics in *Beverly Hills Cop*.

In the *Beverly Hills Cop* movies, the situations are played straight and humor arises out of instances of "Eddie just being Eddie." This is an easier conceit in a movie like Beverly Hills Cop, where the entire premise is based around the culture-clash of a streetwise Detroit cop dealing with the lunacy of life in Southern California. Humor comes from conflict and that conflict is baked into the story just by virtue of the premise. A good example is the moment in *Beverly Hills Cop II* where Murphy's Axel Foley has to talk his way into a Playboy Mansion party to confront a criminal. To get past the receptionist, Axel pretends to be a pool man and improvises a routine about being sent there to clean up an embarrassing spill. It's a silly bit, but it plays off of an obstacle placed in Foley's path. He needs to get into that party and this is how he goes about it.

A similar moment later in that same film comes when he has to confront an accountant played by Gilbert Gottfried. Axel needs to use his computer so he can access some information on the bad guys. The way he achieves this is by showing up pretending to arrest Gottfried for hundreds of dollars in unpaid parking tickets and inducing him to give Axel a bribe. Then he claims he needs access to the man's computer in order to clear the tickets. Sure, there's some silliness, but it gets some genuine laughs out of Murphy and Gottfried riffing off of each other. More importantly, there's story advancement that comes via the gag.

Bad Boys brand of humor isn't integrated as well into the main storyline. Some gags land well, such as when Marcus needs to convince Lowrey's doorman to let him into Lowrey's apartment. Most of the jokes based around the identity switch, however, don't. Lowrey and Burnett keep up the charade for Julie's benefit long after it seems necessary. They even go to the extreme of switching homes, telling Marcus's wife that he needs to go out of town while Lowrey crashes there. This climaxes later with a joke built around a misunderstood phone call that has Marcus assuming that Lowrey is sleeping with his wife.

If you find yourself asking, "What does any of this have to do with the stolen heroin and the witness they need to protect?" you're raising a question the filmmakers could have stood to scrutinize themselves. The joke moments like this one play like an unwelcome intrusion on what emerges as an action thriller.

I have a theory about this disconnect. Perhaps Bay (or the producers, though they were the ones who bought and developed this script as a comedy) recognized the humor wasn't working and attempted to compensate by amping up the action and violence. This resulted in a film that feels more real than say, *Clean Slate* or *Trapped in Paradise*, to name two Dana Carvey comedy vehicles of that era. In the original version of the script, the one that courted the former *Saturday Night Live* players, it's possible that the identity swap was more of centerpiece and the bad guys were merely fops to facilitate this. The movie *Sister Act* uses a similar concept when Whoopi Goldberg's character witnesses a mob hit and has to hide out in a convent. The balance of the film is her fish-out-of-water experience while pretending to be a nun. Even though the bad guys show up to provide some jeopardy and a kidnapping in the third act, they're handled with a light touch. It's not hard to imagine a take on *Bad Boys* that plays in a similar tone. (Whether such a film would be entertaining is another question entirely.)

The casting would seem to support this intention. Remember, in 1995 Will Smith and Martin Lawrence were sitcom stars. This might be the equivalent of casting Andy Samberg and Aziz Ansarai in the present. Sometimes, the tone of a rewrite follows the essence of the star. (To invoke *Beverly Hills Cop* again, it was at one point written for Sylvester Stallone. The casting of Eddie Murphy changed that movie entirely.) With comedy actors on board, that's probably not where we should point the fingers.

So again we return to Bay as the likely force behind the film's tonal shift. Based only on this film, it would be probable that such a refiguring was deliberate. However, Bay has never shown much deftness with humor in many of his later films and it's possible that he wasn't yet adept enough to use these comedic talents to their full potential. As this was still early in Will Smith's career, he hadn't yet honed his onscreen persona.

In a *GQ* profile of Bay, Smith recalls a sequence that helped the actor remold his image as a sex symbol. The director implored his star to perform a critical chase scene with his shirt open. Smith rebuffed at first, calling it "corny," but he'd soon recant after he understood what Bay was doing. "That was the moment for me where I learned how important single images are. That single image took me from a comedic television actor to a potential movie star. The scripts that I started to get offered changed dramatically." It transformed him from a funny guy to a sex symbol, and that in turn defined the rest of Smith's career.

A year later, a different director would help him burst off the screen to steal *Independence Day* and galvanize the image Will Smith: The Icon. There's a natural ease, confidence, and charisma to many of Smith's later performances that isn't entirely formed here. He's good, but he doesn't dominate. Yet it's impossible to deny that what Bay did for Smith represents a giant leap in his career.

Still other evidence suggests that perhaps Bay's voice was modulated by his collaborators. Stylistically, the film doesn't look like "a Michael Bay film" through-out most of it. While it could be assumed this is because his aesthetic was still developing, one need only look at his video for Meat Loaf's "I Would Do Anything for Love (But I Won't Do That)" to see the Bay hallmarks of saturated oranges, camera spins, and curvy scantily-clad women were in place two years before *Bad Boys* was released.

Most later-day Bay films are crawling with women who look like they stepped out of a Victoria's Secret ad or a rap video. As much as Bay favors that aesthetic for his leading ladies, he really enjoys that motif for his extras too. That this film is set in Miami would seem to provide the perfect backdrop for "Michael Bay women." Strangely enough, that eye candy is restrained. It only really cuts loose during a sequence at a party near the middle of the film.

While Tea Leoni is an attractive woman, in a line-up of Michael Bay leading ladies, she would appear quite out of place. She was 29 at the time of release, making her the oldest leading lady of literally every other Michael Bay movie except for *Bad Boys II*. On top of that, her wardrobe and make-up are more conservative than most other Bay-ladies, drastically so when compared with several women from later in Bay's career. Her character is stuck in the role of the "woman who needs to be protected," but Leoni at least imbues her with some spunk and ends up giving the impression that this woman has a little more agency than the women who frequent action films of this sort.

The villains fail to leave much of an impression, again recalling the sorts of villains who populated the *Beverly Hills Cop* series, though without the edges and the compelling performers who could make an impression alongside Eddie Murphy. This could be another holdover from the more comedic inception of the project, when the bad guys could have been less defined as antagonists and few would care so long as the jokes kept flying.

Another instance of holdover '80s quaintness is the simple fact that these two leads are merely cops trying to solve a case. Today, this would be rejected as too pedestrian, not enough of a high concept. One of the cops would have to be a psychic, or an alien from a planet where heroin was medicine and he needs to recover the 100 pounds of the drug to save his race. Of course, there's always the theory that the theft was perpetrated by evil time travelers looking to alter the future, but I personally find that premise to be a bit obvious.

This film is an anomaly in Bay's career in many ways and my personal theory is that Don Simpson has something to do with that. Simpson was a large personality and it's very reasonable to conclude that there wasn't enough room on this production for two aggressive egos. If nothing else, a man as forceful as Simpson is clearly capable of running roughshod over a first-time feature director, even if that director is Michael Bay. If this is what happened, it would cast an interesting light on Bay's later collaborations with Bruckheimer following Simpson's passing.

On the commentary, Bay complains about never having enough time or money to shoot the action scenes the way he wanted to shoot them. "We had $10,000 for a rewrite, and we had to go let the writer go play golf every day, that was part of the deal," he said to *The Los Angeles Times* in 2009. "No one believed in the script. Don Simpson and Jerry Bruckheimer were working on *Crimson Tide*, that was their real movie, we were the tiny movie on the side."

With so much stacked against him, this imposed the same sorts of limitations on him that some of the aforementioned auteur filmmakers dealt with on their signature films. The difference here is that Bay had to work within those limitations while being beholden to another voice, his producers. Thus, the completed film is likely vastly different from what Bay would have done if given the autonomy he enjoyed for much of the rest of his career.

The situation is not unlike the one faced by David Fincher on the third *Alien* film. (Interesting, both Fincher and Bay were associated with the music video and film production company Propaganda Films early in their careers as music video directors.) Fincher famously clashed with the studio over the film and was left feeling like the producers didn't defend him. He lost several battles during the making of that movie and was the only director not to contribute to the *Alien Anthology* DVD and blu-ray release. Over the years, Fincher has been fairly blunt about hating the picture and has all but disowned it. A semblance of his vision was released on the same box set under the title "The Assembly Cut," but it seems likely that only represents a fraction of what Fincher was trying to achieve.

Bay ended up paying for one critical scene himself, explaining in a *GQ* interview, After clashing with studio executives who wouldn't front the cash to have Martin Lawrence shot a bad guy out of a plane, Bay reached into his own pocket to the tune of $25,000. He claims he wasn't reimbursed until after the film made $60 million. In the same *GQ* profile, Bruckheimer recalls Bay's dedication throughout the shoot. On the first day, Bay did 40 set-ups, which Bruckheimer says is four times as many as an average director manages. He had to hustle; the film's budget was only $19 million.

Alas, there is no equivalent to Fincher's *Alien 3* assembly cut for Bay's freshman effort. *Bad Boys'* legacy might have been to be the hard knocks that would motivate Bay to fight harder for his vision on future projects. Much as *Alien 3* is less Fincher's true coming out than *Se7en* would be, *Bad Boys* is not so much "a Michael Bay film" as it is an interesting artifact of several different turning points in film history. It is the beginning of what appeared to be a revival of the Simpson/Bruckheimer style of blockbuster, as well as – though no one knew it at the time – the start of the passing of the torch from Don Simpson to Michael Bay as Jerry Bruckheimer's close collaborator. It's also the first stages of Will Smith's transformation into summer movie superstar. It's a project where many of the players are in either their nascent stages or on the precipice of decline.

This movie might have made Bay a feature director, but it wouldn't be until his next film that he would become an auteur.

The Rock (1996)

Release date: June 7, 1996
Story by David Weisberg & Douglas S. Cook
Screenplay by David Weisberg & Douglas S. Cook and Mark Rosner
Produced by Don Simpson, Jerry Bruckheimer
Budget: $75 million
Domestic box office: $134 million
Global box office: $335 million

Every iconic filmmaker has that movie that is not their first production, but the one that will dominate their filmography for the rest of their careers. For these truly brilliant directors, that masterpiece usually arrives within their first three films. Steven Spielberg had *Jaws*, George Lucas had *Star Wars*, Quentin Tarantino had *Pulp Fiction*, and David Fincher had *Se7en*. For Michael Bay, that movie is *The Rock*.

Whether or not *The Rock* is Bay's absolute best film may be a matter of debate. It happens to be my personal favorite. When I want a film that will challenge me and make me think, I of course will reach for *Transformers: Age of Extinction*. As we have discussed, that film easily represents a creative pinnacle in3 Bay's career. But when I'm in the mood for something with a less political bent and more rollicking good fun, I reach for *The Rock*.

Though Michael Bay is without peer, as I examine this film, I of course find myself paralleling him with Steven Soderbergh.

Soderbergh burst onto the indie film scene in 1989 with *Sex, Lies, and Videotape* and spent over the next decade becoming known for unusual indie films outside the mainstream. It would not be until 2000's Julia Roberts vehicle *Erin Brockovich* that Soderbergh would truly make a mainstream film with a major star. But even then, one could argue that its status as a true-life Oscar bait film salvaged Soderbergh's reputation. No one would dare call it slumming to direct a film that won America's Sweetheart her first Oscar.

This is why it was still jarring when Soderbergh dove headfirst into big-budget, star-driven, genre filmmaking with *Ocean's Eleven* just a year later. With a cast that included superstars George Clooney and Brad Pitt, this remake of the 1960 Rat Pack film aspired to be nothing more than a fun romp. It was the pinnacle of studio filmmaking, elevated by the technical skill and keen directorial hand of the auteur. *Ocean's Eleven* will probably never be named first when cinephiles are debating what his best film is, but that doesn't take away from how perfectly structured, masterfully performed and expertly executed it is. It's certainly among the best in its genre. What *Ocean's Eleven* represents to Soderbergh, *The Rock* represents to Michael Bay. Yes, we know that deep down, Bay is capable of far more complicated work than this, but that doesn't diminish the accomplishments of *The Rock* any more.

Many of Bay's later productions saw him being brought on in the early stages, sometimes developing the screenplay from the ground up. That is not the case with *The Rock*, which began life as a screenplay from David Weisberg & Douglas F. Cook. It was originally bought by Disney for Caravan Pictures, but found its way to Simpson/Bruckheimer. They commissioned rewrites and by the time the script made it to screen, at least seven writers had their crack at it, including Mark Rosner and Aaron Sorkin. However, Bay's closest collaborator was Jonathan Hensleigh, who was denied screen credit following a Writers Guild of America arbitration proceeding. (Bay would later write an open letter to the Guild in *The Los Angeles Times* decrying the verdict.)

Still, the point is that this was not a project initiated by Bay so much as it was reshaped by his influence. The result was a compelling thrill-ride that showed how good an action movie Bay could make even when coloring within the lines on a killer high-concept premise. The hook: tourists on Alcatraz Island have been taken by rogue Brigadier General Frank Hummel (Ed Harris), a decorated war hero with an entire group of U.S. Marines on his side. They threaten to deadly VX-Gas at San Francisco if their demands are not met - $100 million paid to the families of soldiers who were killed on secret missions, soldiers whose families never got compensation.

To get onto "the Rock," the Pentagon and the FBI need to recruit the only man ever to successfully escape Alcatraz, John Mason. Mason – played by Sean Connery – is a British spy that they've been holding for the better part of 30 years. Mason and chemical weapons expert Stanley Goodspeed (Nicolas Cage) are sent to the island with a SEAL team in order to lead them through the same security measures and uncharted tunnels Mason himself used to escape back in 1963. Unfortunately, the entire SEAL team is killed upon arrival and it falls to the British spy and Goodspeed – who's never been in the field before – to stop the missiles and end the hostage situation.

This is flat-out one of the best premises Bay has had to work with in his career. It's such a good premise that it would have been easy to get lazy in the execution and simply coast on the hook. However, even as Bay amps up the scale of the action scenes, he introduces a lot of depth in places where we don't expect it.

One of the most critical and subversive moves of the film is that it introduces the "villain" first. Hummel has some humanizing moments at a military funeral and then at his wife's grave. It's a very deliberate decision to not have his first scene be the more conventional entrance when he leads the team on a raid to steal chemical weapons, or later when the team seizes control of the island. A lesser film would see Hummel as a plot device, just an antagonistic force to motivate Mason and Goodspeed onto the island. Here, he's allowed to be a human, complicated character. He's possibly the most multi-dimensional of any of Bay's antagonists.

Harrris's performance sells Hummel as a man who commands respect the instant he walks into a room. You believe this is a man who has made his bones in the military. There's no effort at making him into a lunatic or a suave, wise-cracking madman, as so many action villains are. He's there to do a job and he's fully accepted the consequences of that task. Further cementing him as the anti-Hans Gruber is the moment just before taking hostages where he tells kids from a school group that they should find their teacher and get back to the mainland. He needs hostages, but he's not putting kids in harm's way needlessly.

It presents an interesting dilemma to the viewer. Is Hummel wrong? Do we even want to see him fail? Of course, the U.S. government cannot give in to terrorism, so Hummel and the military are on an unstoppable collision course. Even when Hummel's men kill the SEAL team, it doesn't tarnish our view of him. He first tries to get them to surrender and when a sudden crashing spooks Hummel's men, they open fire and kill all the SEALs before the confusion is sorted out. It's clear Hummel finds this regrettable, but from his perspective, these men were enemy combatants who made the confrontation necessary.

With all the possible motivations and villains Bay could have chosen, this was the one he was drawn to. This version of Hummel was the one who emerged after seven writers, many more drafts, and a lot of reshaping of the script over years. It's no accident or whim that Hummel was developed like this. After later films like *Pearl Harbor* and *Transformers*, Bay got tagged as a very pro-military artist. While that's not necessarily untrue, Bay's willingness to criticize the military through the character of Hummel shows that he's not the military hawk/stooge he's often painted as. It's rare to see this direct a criticism of the military, but one should remember this was made pre-9/11, in the peacetime days of the Clinton Administration. The attacks on the World Trade Center would change much of the culture, including Bay's films.

It's also possible to read into this film a criticism of America's foreign policy. Though most of Hummel's team is made up of soldiers he's directly served under, some of them, like Tony Todd's Captain Darrow, are new to his unit. Darrow and a few of his men take to their role as mercenaries perhaps too easily. They're younger than Hummel and less disciplined than the career military man. While Hummel sees his actions as a regrettable necessity, Darrow and his men appear almost thrilled at the prospect of committing violence. Every step of the way, they are the unstable force pushing Hummel to commit more reckless and violent acts. It suddenly becomes clear why supervillains like Lex Luthor tend to employ henchmen who are merely benign idiots rather than trigger-happy head-cases.

This conflict comes to a head when Hummel cannot bring himself to execute a hostage and then ensures that a rocket he launched gets redirected out to sea before it detonates. Realizing he's been beaten, the leader calls for an abort to the mission, but Darrow and two other men revolt when they realize this means they won't be paid for their efforts. A Mexican standoff ensues and when the dust settles, Hummel is dead and it's up to Mason and Goodspeed to find and stop the final rocket before the other men can launch it.

Is Bay making a statement about the military of old and the military of the present? The old guard joined up because they believed in honor and patriotism. Their values would not allow them to harm civilians. The military that Darrow represents is a blunt instrument, concerned only with their own self-interests. When those interests align with the military, things go well, but honor and pragmatism seem not to dictate the mission.

This challenging of a black-and-white past with a more complicated present is a theme continued via the character of James Mason. This British spy has been locked up since the Cold War because he stole some of J. Edgar Hoover's most prized secrets. As one of the film's more arch lines tells us, "This man knows our most intimate secrets from the last half century! The alien landing at Roswell, the truth behind the J.F.K. assassination. Mason's angry, he's lethal, he's a trained killer... and he is the only hope that we have got!"

It's left to the viewer to weigh the morality there. Mason might have stolen secrets, but it was on behalf of a government that was not in conflict with the U.S. then. Further, we're reminded that these secrets were cultivated by J. Edgar Hoover, who "kept secret files on prominent Americans and Europeans. De Gaulle, British members of Parliament, even the Prime Minister… this guy had dirt on everybody in the world." That this isn't a simple black-and-white matter feels very deliberate, as campy as it is to claim that aliens actually came to Earth and that there's a JFK conspiracy that was known all along.

Remember, Mason escaped Alcatraz in 1963 and there was only one month and eight days left in that year after JFK was shot. The implication is that either Mason discovered the truth about the assassination very soon after it happened, was caught quickly and then escaped just as swiftly… or somehow, he uncovered the conspiracy before the assassination. In fact, that is the only scenario that's possible because the prison itself was ordered closed on March 21, 1963. The script tap-dances around this, but the larger implication seems to be that the Kennedy Assassination was a government conspiracy that, at a minimum, Hoover knew about long before it took place.

And people think that Bay can't be subtle when he wants to be.

One also cannot discount the obvious connections between Connery's character and his iconic role as James Bond. It's fairly easy to read Mason as a stand-in for James Bond himself. In his prime, he was skilled enough to escape difficult incarceration at least once, but likely more. (His Alcatraz escape happened in 1963, but his daughter was conceived in the mid-1970s. This suggests either he was on the run for a decade, or that he was recaptured soon after Alcatraz and then sprang himself again at a later date.)

On one hand, it's an expression of incredible patriotism to depict that America was able to keep James Bond behind bars for most of the last 30 years. On the other hand, these are the men who stopped James Bond from preventing a Presidential assassination. *The Rock* takes place in an alternate reality where James Bond failed and the bad guys won. It's a dark slap in the face to the escapist nature of the '60s spy films. That Bay buries all of this subtext inside of what appears to be a mere casting in-joke only underlines how much brilliance permeates this film.

The only explanation for how *The Rock* failed to achieve an Academy Award nomination in the face of such brilliance and political criticism that the Academy was unaccustomed to finding such depth in a simple action film. The five nominees that year were *The English Patient*, *Fargo*, *Jerry Maguire*, *Secrets & Lies*, and *Shine*. It was clearly a year where the Academy made a point of rejecting conventional Hollywood films, and only a bias against the genre, Bay and Simpson/Bruckheimer can be responsible for the omission here.

Fortunately critics were not so blind. Roger Ebert gave the film three and a half stars, saying, "Director Michael Bay ("Bad Boys") orchestrates the elements into an efficient and exciting movie, with some big laughs, sensational special effects sequences, and sustained suspense."

Ebert's praise of Cage is not misplaced. The actor's Stanley Goodspeed is a true anomaly in the Bay canon: a leading man who isn't a man's-man. The everyman is not a frequent visitor to Bay's world, and more often than not, that type is treated as the comic relief. (*Transformers*' Sam Witwicky might also be a notable exception.) Goodspeed is not a field agent, he's a chemical expert with the FBI who happens to be in the right place to get caught up in the Mason situation. His knowledge of the chemical weapons means he's drafted into the field, making him a true fish-out-of-water.

What works about this is that Goodspeed's more nerdy qualities aren't just there to make Mason look more masculine by contrast. Goodspeed is allowed to handle himself pretty well for a novice, where other films might have turned him into an annoying sidekick that the British spy was saddled with. This is a true two-hander, with both men earning each other's respect. Two early interactions sell this. The first is Goodspeed's interrogation of Mason, where he stammers nervously until eventually trying to put on a tough guy act. Mason's bemusement at this unpolished agent actually helps humanize the prisoner a bit. As his gentlemanly tone starts to win over Goodspeed, it has the effect of disarming the audience as well. It's a deft ballet that both characters emerge from more fully developed.

The second moment comes a bit later after Mason's provoked a chase through San Francisco. He arranges a meeting with the daughter he's never seen before. Goodspeed figures this out and calls in Mason's location. As Mason concludes his chat with his daughter, several police cars pull up. The daughter recoils, assuming that her father broke out of jail and these men are here to take him back. Goodspeed allows Mason to preserve some dignity, saying that he's with the government and "Your father is helping us to resolve a dangerous situation." The audience thinks better of Goodspeed for doing Mason that kindness and Mason's appreciation of the same also conveys that he recognizes the significance of this as well. With those moments out of the way, the stage is set for the film to become a true two-hander.

Cage is the perfect actor for Goodspeed, perfectly deploying his manic energy. He's able to sell Goodspeed's nervousness when he's out of his element and then quickly shift to his authority when he's on familiar terrain. To wit, there's a scene where a still-twitching body unnerves him, but then a minute later, he has no problem snapping at Mason when he fears Mason's ignorance of the chemical weapons might accidentally kill all of them. Cage's performance allows Goodspeed to have some "action hero moments" without compromising his everyman qualities. Mason could not have stopped the bad guys by himself and the film is wise to make Goodspeed every bit as integral to the situation as the British spy is. Bay takes a "normal guy" and evolves the film to the point that he's able to shoot him like a hero. It's a welcome change from the then-current Schwarzenegger and Stallone action types who sprung to the screen as fully formed bad-asses, akin to Athena bursting forth from Zeus's skull. When it comes to the characters in *The Rock*, Hummel has depth, Mason has charisma, but it's Goodspeed who has the true character arc. A character like that is the key to an effective action film.

This would also seem to be the place to take stock of how the women fare in this Bay outing. This is a very testosterone-heavy film, with only two women of any real significance. One of these is Mason's daughter, who only appears in one scene and is more significant for how she motivates Mason than for any agency of her own. The second is Goodspeed's pregnant fiancé Carla. She too has little significance beyond giving Stanley an emotional tie outside the mission. As played by Vanessa Marcil, she's got a little spunk to her, even proposing to Stanley when she realizes she's pregnant. However, she makes little impact on the plot.

It is worth noting that neither of them yet conform to the prototypical "Bay-type" of woman. As attractive as both actresses are, they are dressed like regular women, not rock video extras. There's no undue leering at their curves and neither one conveys the idea that they exist largely to be eye candy. Eventually, the supermodel-in-a-music-video female visualization will become a Bay staple, but not yet with this film.

This film was also the first true translation of Bay's music-video aesthetic to feature film. The camera is frequently in motion from shot to shot even as the pacing of the shots is exceptionally fast. The "Trivia" section for this film on the Internet Movie Database claims that there are about 2900 shots in the two hour and six minute running time. The average shot length is 2.6 seconds and the median shot length is 2.5 seconds. I recall at the time, some viewers complained that the film itself seemed to have Attention Deficit Disorder, but it's hard to deny that it doesn't make for a powerful viewing experience.

With this film, Michael Bay changed the look and pacing of the action film forever. James Cameron had been the reigning god of action films up to this point, but going forward, Bay's influence would become more apparent in the works of Brett Ratner, Peter Berg and Simon West.

In 2011, *Variety* senior film critic Peter Debruge said, "Michael Bay has recognized the energy of an action sequence can replace the logic of it… By getting in there and mixing up the angles, he creates the same sense of excitement and confusion through editing and camera placement that you would if you were actually in the fight."

Perhaps intentionally invoking Bay's history as a commercial director, Debruge put his finger on the method of the Bay aesthetic, "If you look at a Michael Bay movie, you're watching 2 1/2 hours of money shots and quotable tag lines. Every shot is designed to send tingles up your spine. When I watch a Michael Bay feature, I feel like I'm watching a full-length trailer."

This sort of visual style is critical to decoding every Michael Bay film. It began in *The Rock* and continues throughout all of his other films, no matter the subject matter. The story and subject bend to Michael Bay, not the other way around. In many ways, he's the purest embodiment of the auteur theory.

The commentary on *The Rock* offers further examples of Bay's meticulousness and his understanding of his audience. In the second half-hour of the film, Mason makes an escape attempt and leads a massive car chase through the streets of San Francisco. It's a good opportunity for Bay to blow up cars and even a trolley, though by the end of the sequence, Mason is back in the hands of the authorities. Explaining his motivation for this, Bay says:

"Actually, I had a fight about the car chase with one of the writers, because I felt his is a way for me to help, after all this complicated setup, to help suck the younger audience back into it… one of the writers said 'I've never heard of a director talking about demographics.'" Bay says he gave him a simple answer "If you're given 60 million dollars, you'd better fucking know who you're selling this movie to, because it could be the last time they ever give you 60 million dollars again."

An audience will forgive a lot if they are enjoying themselves. Bay understands this like no other. So much of his visual language is built around triggering certain emotional responses and touchstones. Other artists try to achieve this connection with their audience through a strict adherence to story logic and meticulous visual coherency. What Bay comprehends is that this inherent order is a lie. Film is a symphony of emotion, and if you as an artist know the right stimulus/response buttons to trigger, you can evoke that experience without being dependent on the old "rules."

Certainly Bay makes movies he wants to see, but buried within that desire is a yearning to make movies that the audience will enjoy. Because of this, it's tempting to affix him with the label of "Sell-Out," but ultimately, his concern is with customer satisfaction. Elsewhere on the commentary, he talks about how he observes an audience during his test screenings: "When they start to fidget, when they start to look at their watch, you know you've got a problem with your film."

Michael Bay's films are designed for audiences. They are built for that theatre experience and his obsessive determination to get this right marks him as a true showman in this business. *The Rock* is a film that can please on superficial levels, but still carries enough weight to appeal to those viewers hoping to find something deeper. It is a banquet for all appetites, and Michael Bay is dedicated to ensuring everyone has all they can eat.

Armageddon (1998)

Release date: July 1, 1998
Story by Robert Roy Pool and Jonathan Hensleigh
Adaptation by Tony Gilroy and Shane Salerno
Screenplay by Jonathan Hensleigh and J.J. Abrams
Produced by Michael Bay, Jerry Bruckheimer, Gale Anne Hurd
Budget: $140 million
Domestic box office: $201.6 million
Global box office: $352.1 million

Art is often inexorably linked to the time in which it is produced. Though much art can transcend that context, one often derives greater appreciation and understanding by examining the world that birthed it. It is possible to enjoy *Invasion of the Body Snatchers* as a simple science-fiction B-movie, but the story and themes of everyday people being replaced by emotionless, alien "pod people" takes on greater resonance when you understand it came at the height of the Communist "Red Scare." Some see it as a commentary on McCarthyism and conformity, while others read into it the fear of Communists hiding among us, indistinguishable from the real thing.

There is some debate as to if this connection was intentional on the part of the artists (on the DVD, star Kevin McCarthy claims that no one involved with the film was trying to make a political commentary.) I'm of the personal opinion that an artist doesn't always have to consciously place themes in their work in order for those ideas to be there. Any act of creation is bound to be subject to subconscious influences. It's also not so great a leap to imagine that the fears and concerns of an era end up being transformed into allegories as an author is tapping into their own terrors in an effort to impact an audience.

This is what we need to keep in mind when examining what may very well be Michael Bay's *Citizen Kane*, nay, his *Intolerance* – a little film called *Armageddon*.

Science fiction is frequently a conduit for the social fears of the time. Just as *Invasion of the Body Snatchers* drew on communism, *The Day the Earth Stood Still* was about the fears of the atomic era in the wake of the bombings of Hiroshima and Nagasaki. That is why an examination of *Armageddon* cannot properly begin without recalling its Clinton-era genesis. The "evil Empire" was long gone, the Berlin Wall pulverized, the economy expanding and the tech bubble still inflating. In an age of prosperity, with the Cold War over and no Middle East wars, what did we have to fear?

Judgment.

This was an all-too-brief age when we were no longer concerned that we would bring about our own end. It was an optimistic era in which children did not go to school to learn duck-and-cover, nor did they fear that some politician with his finger on the button would be the instigator of their extermination. The greatest threat to mankind no longer seemed to be man-made, but rather a potential act of God.

The opening sequence of *Armageddon* brings this home, as Charlton Heston's voiceover narrates the demise of the dinosaurs due to an asteroid impact on Earth over 65 million years ago. "This is the Earth, at a time when the dinosaurs roamed a lush and fertile planet. A piece of rock just 6 miles wide changed all that. It hit with the force of 10,000 nuclear weapons. A trillion tons of dirt and rock hurtled into the atmosphere, creating a suffocating blanket of dust the sun was powerless to penetrate for a thousand years. It happened before. It will happen again. It's just a question of when."

Never underestimate Charlton Heston's capacity to scare the shit out of an audience. It's a function he would repeat just a year later when he spoke at an NRA convention just days after the Columbine school shootings.

Armageddon was birthed by this fear. (Judgment, not school shootings. As of yet, Michael Bay has yet to tackle that hot button topic.) It's not a stretch in the slightest to call this Michael Bay's most religious and spiritual work. As an element that mankind takes no responsibility for and cannot control, the meteor is God. It is a dispassionate, unyielding force about to rain judgment upon mankind just as it did the dinosaurs when their time in existence had run its course. It's no accident the film is called "*Armageddon*," derived from the Book of Revelation, the site of the amassing of armies for the end times. Presumably, Bay meant no connection to the 1970s hard rock supergroup of the same name, though I admit they fall outside my usual aural tastes and that perhaps I have neglected yet another possible layer to this already dense film.

Beginning with the understanding that the meteor is God, the most reasonable interpretation of the film's central thesis is that Man has to destroy God in order to survive judgment. This makes it even more telling that the weapons called upon in this final battle are the tools of NASA and a nuclear bomb. These are some of the most notable products of the atomic age: the space race and nuclear proliferation. It is both correct and potent that the only arrows in the quiver that are of any value are technology. Only science can slay God.

(This makes me wonder if the winners of the Nobel Prize in Physics thank God when they reach the podium.)

Indeed, one might even extrapolate that the film's implicit message is that Mankind cannot endure until it rejects God and demonstrates fealty to science. Politics and religion are deeply intertwined, both in this film and in life in general. Those on the right-wing end of the political spectrum are more frequently associated with Christian values. In the years since this film was made, that connection has only become more pronounced even as the political camps of Democrat and Republican have become more polarized. Recent polls place the blame for this post-September 11th shift with Bush, the British rock band that disappeared from the music scene around 2002.

Thus the casting of Bruce Willis, one of the most notable Hollywood Republicans, as the hero of this film cannot be considered an accident. The film takes care to demonstrate that his character, Harry Stamper's, politics are likely aligned with Willis's own. Not only is driller Stamper introduced on an oil rig – thus associating him with a typically Republican industry – but his first act is to gleefully fling golf balls at Greenpeace protestors (a liberal organization, obviously.) And what is the absolute demands that Stamper and his men make of the U.S. Government? "None of them wanna pay taxes again. Ever." Suffice to say, that's a very "red state" demand. Presumably cut are the scenes of him listening to Rush Limbaugh and shouting "Mega dittos!" while checking the schedule for the G. Gordon Liddy book signing.

Throughout the film, there are subtle inferences that Harry Stamper is a man of God. More than once in the script, he calls upon God for help, most notably when he says, "Come on, God, just a little help. It's all I'm asking" when the clock is ticking and the success of their mission is in doubt.

For the sake of argument, allow me to draw parallels and contrasts between Harry Stamper and the story of Job. (I realize this may be an obvious connection, but for the sake of thoroughness and at the risk of insulting your intelligence, I will unpack it somewhat.) Job was a devout servant of God until the Lord removed his protection of Job as a test, allowing Satan to beset him with all manner of calamities. This robbed him of his wealth, his health and even his own children. And yet that still didn't shake Job's faith. That's how strong his devotion was – it even withstood the sacrifice of his children.

In the film, Harry has a daughter named Grace, played by Liv Tyler. Grace has been carrying on a secret affair with Ben Affleck's A.J., whom Harry later says he always considered a son. Early in the movie, we see the circumstances of how Harry learns his daughter has been sleeping with A.J., as he finds her in his bed. Harry's response is a mature one – he grabs a shotgun and proceeds to chase A.J. all over the oil rig, taking nearly a half-dozen shots at him. ("Make your peace with God, A.J.," he shouts.) Though he later plays this off as joking around, it seems clear that in that moment he intended to do him serious harm and was indifferent to the potential that his shots could have killed him. (I personally am an Affleck fan, but those of you who are not should feel free to insert your anti-Affleck jokes here. I might suggest one based on the premise that Harry's clean misses serve as evidence that there is no God, or that at the very least, he is indifferent.)

Now consider the climax of the film. The drillers have completed digging an 800 foot hole into the asteroid. All that remains is to leave the nuclear device in it, except that the remote detonator isn't working. One of the team will have to stay behind and sacrifice themselves to set off the bomb. Harry's men draw straws to see who stays and A.J. "wins." Essentially, Harry is being asked to sacrifice his "son" to "God" (the asteroid.) If he were as faithful as Job, Harry would leave him to that fate.

But that's not what happens. Harry accompanies A.J. outside the ship, then damages A.J.'s air supply and forces A.J. back inside the airlock. Here he takes A.J.'s place as the one who will set off the bomb and save Earth. If the message of *Armageddon* is that science is the tool that will allow man to destroy God, then it surely is significant that ultimately it is a man of God who is called upon to slay God, even as he acts in direct opposition to the meaning of the Book of Job. The boy Harry would have slain at the start of the film has become the boy he saves, underscoring his arc and the inversion of his values. It seems that Bay is saying that for mankind to endure, it must evolve and leave the old traditions behind.

Lest you think that to be too far of a reach, there are grounds for considering Michael Bay a prophet. The Bible was dictated from God to Moses and became a story that was passed down orally before being eventually transcribed and translated by many writers. Reflect upon that when you realize that this was the first film Bay made where he had significant input into the story at its inception.

As he discusses on the commentary, Bay had a deal for another film after the success of *The Rock*. The only problem was that neither Disney nor Bruckheimer Films had any scripts he was interested in directing. So he reached out to Johnathan Hensleigh, who had done a great deal of work on *The Rock,* and this was the idea that emerged from their story sessions. Eventually it would be worked on by many subsequent writers, allowing Bay to speak through multiple voices until the delivery to the public at large was refined.

Did Bay intend this as a religious parable? That's a much harder judgment to make, and ultimately it doesn't matter. As we have discussed, the unconscious mind has a way of investing a story with subliminal resonance that the author may not consciously be aware of. There is an outside chance that the first time Michael Bay learns that he is a prophet will arrive when he eventually reads this book. My personal assumption is that his own values clearly infiltrated the story, whether that was his greatest motivation or not.

However there are some prescient elements in this film that do give weight to the idea that Bay's creative process got a helping hand from a higher power. An early sequence in the film features the destruction of the space shuttle Atlantis in orbit. Nearly five years after this film was released, on February 1, 2003, the space shuttle *Columbia* was destroyed in a disaster as it re-entered Earth's atmosphere. Though the circumstances are extremely different, that didn't stop hoaxers from using *Armageddon* footage and trying to pass it off as actual video of the tragedy. This could be a simple coincidence or perhaps an indication we should be scouring this film and other Bay films for dark portents of what lies ahead.

What might be more significant is that the initial meteorite impacts in New York produce devastation that eerily echoes that which resulted from the attack on the World Trade Center's twin towers on September 11, 2001. The visualization of that destruction seemed far-fetched at the time, but with hindsight, so resembled the attacks that would arrive three years later that on that fateful day. On September 11 people referred to the sight of the towers collapsing as "like something out of a Michael Bay film." The fantastic had been made real as current events validated Michael Bay as a visionary in more ways than one.

(What's notable about this is that only the New York attack exhibits this level of verisimilitude. The destruction of Shanghai and Paris both look exceptionally fake by today's visual effects standards. Perhaps this is because their inclusion did not spring from Bay's prognostications and thus he had to visually invent them out of whole cloth.)

It's hard to ignore that the intervening years haven't been kind to the VFX in general, though. At the time, they were state of the art, but in all probability the computing power that got this film done is probably equal to whatever was used on *Sharknado*. This is somewhat analogous to the fact that the computing power that got us to the moon is now exceeded by your average cell phone. The upside of this is that should we ever return to lunar exploration, our brave astronauts will be able to advance through Candy Crush even as their spacecraft is captured by the moon's gravity.

The *Sharknado* comparison is an apt one in more ways than one, as both projects exist purely for and were discovered by people who go to the movies just for the sheer pleasure of those moving images and heightened emotions. Experiencing *Armageddon* purely on this surface level, one can understand how it plays to that particular audience. This is often expounded upon in terms of Bay's ability to reach a "middle American" audience.

What's remarkable is that even as that audience is swept away by the iconic lead actor, the murderer's row of excellent supporting players, and the truly intense visuals and action, the intellectual viewer is able to process all of the themes laid out earlier in this chapter. In speaking to both vastly different audiences at the same time, Michael Bay has made one of the few perfect movies ever in existence. It transcends by far his accomplishment with *The Rock*, where he directed a very gripping action-thriller that stands with the best of that genre. This achievement is not just a victory for sci-fi and action, it's a triumph of both cinema and story-telling in general.

Within this film is Bay's first deconstruction of modern blockbuster. As a visual craftsman, Bay is drawn to the iconography of an image over the functionality of it. It's something that Roger Ebert perceived but failed to properly appreciated in his negative review of the film, in which he wrote "Here it is at last, the first 150-minute trailer. "Armageddon" is cut together like its own highlights. Take almost any 30 seconds at random, and you'd have a TV ad. The movie is an assault on the eyes, the ears, the brain, common sense and the human desire to be entertained."

Bay makes movies that could almost be appreciated as silent films because the visual information is that potent. Understanding this, he further appreciates that the human brain is able to interpret visual input at an astounding speed. In fact, a recent study, conducted by MIT researchers and published in the journal *Attention, Perception, and Psychophysics*, found that the brain can process an image in 13 milliseconds. The Internet Movie Database Trivia entry for the film states that the average cut in this movie lasts about 1.5 seconds. Though Mr. Ebert perceived this to be unusually high, the fact remains it is well within the threshold for the brain to interpret the images. A picture truly is worth more than a thousand words, why not impart those "words" to the audience at a speed with which they can easily keep up? To do otherwise is to risk both boring them and insulting their intelligence.

Even his detractors would be hard-pressed to argue that Bay doesn't know how to sell a hero shot, such as *The Right Stuff* homage of Stamper's men walking towards the camera before embarking on their mission. There's genuine emotion in the staging of Harry's farewell to his daughter, as a bank of monitors displays his face, his daughter reaching out to touch the screen before casting her head down. The shot that follows shows Grace from behind, still palming the screen as it shows only static, our perspective discreetly pulling back from her pain to allow her some privacy. It's impossible to look at those moments and say that Michael Bay doesn't understand filmmaking. Even moreso than *The Rock,* almost every shot here is a money shot, delivering emotion with maximum impact.

In doing so, Bay is able to prove that any seemingly crazy idea can be made emotionally accessible with the proper visual delivery. It helps to remember that the mid-90s was the era of the high concept boom in the spec market place. The spec market had never been hotter, driven by "high concept" stories that could easily be summed up in one sentence: "*Die Hard* on a submarine!" "Stormchasers hunt multiple twisters!" "Dinosaurs are cloned as theme park attractions!" One wonders if Bay was attracted to this story if only to prove that an idea that sounded absurdly far-fetched on its face – oil drillers sent into space to save the Earth from an asteroid – could stir the emotions and bring people to tears. That it also functioned as a fantastic religious parable might only have been icing on the cake. The movie is a triumph of visual iconography over story and plausibility.

Do not think Bay was unaware of the factual inaccuracies in the film. Multiple times on the commentary, he notes where he made a conscious choice to go with the more impactful visual rather than the technically and scientifically "correct" image. In some cases this relates to set-design, as Mission Control appears a lot sleeker on-screen than in real life. "The old Mission Control is the most unsexy thing you've ever seen," he assures the audience. This philosophy also extends to the realities of space travel, as when the Russian space station explodes. Bay notes, "Now I know there's no fire in space, but it is a movie, and most people don't know that." In other cases, the gore that would have resulted from the crashing space craft was muted so that the film would not be slapped with an R-rating.

At least one of the actors also came to understand that factual fidelity was not a priority. In his segment of the commentary, Ben Affleck remarks, "I asked Michael why it was easier to train oil drillers to become astronauts than it was to train astronauts to become oil drillers, and he told me to shut the fuck up, so that was the end of that talk."

True, the entire film hinges on the idea that the Earth's one chance to survive is for a team to land on the asteroid while it's en route to Earth, drill an 800-foot hole into it, drop a nuke in there and detonate it so that it splits neatly into two pieces whose new trajectories will evade Earth. (Smartly, this is explained to the audience in part with a visual simulation rather than through pure exposition, again demonstrating Bay knows what he's doing.) The plot oddity that Affleck refers to above stems from Harry's insistence that the only way he can get this done is with his team, not the astronauts trained to go into space.

As a talented director, Bay realizes that the most essential thing for a film is that the performers communicate that they believe in this scenario. To that end, one of the most important decisions was the casting of Bruce Willis, already an icon of the action-movie everyman, thanks to *Die Hard* and the career that sprang from it. He gives *Armageddon* a strong core to orbit around and is always grounded in every scene. Bay always gets the best results when he either casts icons or makes them.

Much of the rest of the call sheet is made up of some of the finest character actors of that era, each of them called upon to perform as seriously as if they were in the Sundance films that brought them critical acclaim. These include Billy Bob Thornton, Steve Buscemi, William Fichtner, Owen Wilson, Michael Clarke Duncan and Peter Stromare. This is no cheap B-movie cable production and the investment in top-flight talent pays off in spades. The secondary players all become memorable in their own right, with several of them getting quotable lines and distinct personalities.

With regard to the female roles, we still have yet to see the emergence of the traditional "Michael Bay woman." Grace may be played by the fetching Liv Tyler, but the camera refuses to ogle her even though her first appearance comes while disrobed in bed. In the male-dominated atmosphere of NASA, there are barely any women to speak of, though one of the shuttle crew is a woman. ($5 to anyone who can name her without consulting IMDb. $10 to anyone who can say anything significant about her character.) There's also a brief role featuring a stripper, in a sequence that feels like it would be at home in one of Bay's commercials. Not for the first time, we're left with a film where women aren't truly demeaned so much as aggressively underrepresented.

So to nitpick the literal plausibility of the film is to hold it to a standard that few classic films could withstand. Does anyone truly believe that tornado could pluck a Kansas farmhouse from the ground intact and maintain that grip long enough to transport it to a far away land? Surely not, but every school child knows and loves the story of *The Wizard of Oz*. When one watches *Star Wars*, do they pay any notice to the impossibility of faster-than-light travel? Is there even an effort to account for time-dilation? A film's contract with an audience requires only an emotional authenticity, not a literal one.

A key emotional tether for this film is the love affair between A.J. and Grace. Though the commentary claims that this subplot was added in the wake of *Titanic*, that assertion falls apart when one notices that *Titanic* was released on December 19, 1997 and

Armageddon began shooting almost four months earlier, on August 27, 1997, according to the production notes for *Armageddon* on Michael Bay's own website. Though it's possible that *Titanic* script details were known at that early date, the way that film was embraced as a romantic fantasy by teenage girls could not have been predicted in the slightest. Why does Bay give such a different explanation on the commentary? This is likely the legendary Michael Bay modesty at work.

Bay proves himself unashamed to explore different kinds of emotion and love throughout the story. The A.J./Grace romance is just one facet. The movie would not be complete without Harry's fatherly love for Grace, particularly their tearful goodbye. A.J.'s own love and affection for Harry also provides another emotional climax within the film, as Affleck is unafraid to let his emotions show, rather than play it stoically. It's the sort of naked emotion one might more likely find in a silent film, and with that revelation, we again realize that Bay never loses sight of the power of the image. Were it not for the excellent sound design, it might be worth advising viewers to enjoy *Armageddon* with the audio off.

In a behind-the-scenes sense, *Armageddon* marked a new beginning of sorts. Though Michael Bay continued his relationship with super-producer Jerry Bruckheimer, the overseer of his first two films, this was the first project without any input from Bruckheimer's late partner Don Simpson. It would be hard not to argue that Bruckheimer looked to the brash and bombastic Bay to fill the void left by his larger-than-life collaborator. On the film's commentary, Bruckheimer admits he doesn't always agree with Bay, but he puts a lot of trust in his ability to know his audience and deliver what will thrill them.

It is that rare talent that makes *Armageddon* a movie for all audiences. Intellectual, philistine, theologian, and common man alike. Bay's critics often seem to start with the premise that his film's are dumb and then find the "evidence" within the text that props up this claim. True film intellectuals are not blinded by such petty biases. The Criterion Collection blu-ray release contains an essay from noted film historian and Corwin-Fuller Professor of Film Studies and Founder and Curator of The Cinema Archives at Wesleyan University, Jeanine Basinger. She gave the film effusive praise, saying it is "never less than a brilliant mixture of what movies are supposed to do: tell a good story, depict characters through active events, invoke an emotional response, and entertain simply and directly, without pretense."

In addition to her exemplary credentials, Ms. Basinger has made Wesleyan's film program one of the most noted in the country. The distinguished school has many well-known graduates that include New Line Cinema head Toby Emmerich, screenwriters Zak Penn (the *X-Men* films) and Akiva Goldsman (*Batman & Robin*), writer/director Joss Whedon (*Buffy the Vampire Slayer*, *The Avengers*) and director Michael Bay (*Armageddon*.)

I believe that part of the critical backlash to this film is because this is a movie that needs to teach you how to watch it. When it debuted in 1998, there was nothing else quite like it, save for some early examples of Bay's style. However, even this represented a more aggressive approach than *The Rock* had presented to audiences. Perhaps ironically, it's much less difficult to comprehend *Armageddon* after years of ripoffs have made its once-overwhelming aesthetic appear less exemplary. With the Bay-style later emulated by directors such as Peter Berg (*Battleship*) and Stephen Sommers (*G.I. Joe: The Rise of Cobra*), among others, the culture and the audience has caught up to his production style.

Armageddon was Michael Bay's largest and most ambitious effort to-date. It is his magnum opus and a film that gains resonance with each subsequent viewing. Though the critics who scoffed at this film in 1998 would be loathe to admit so, it's not possible to truly explore this film and not come out on the other side with the admission that Michael Bay is a visionary.

Pearl Harbor (2001)

Release date: May 25, 2001
Written by Randall Wallace
Produced by Michael Bay, Jerry Bruckheimer
Budget: $140 million
Domestic box office: $198.5 million
Global box office: $449.2 million

How does a filmmaker follow up perfection?

This was the question facing Michael Bay in the wake of the monster success of *Armageddon*.

As Michael Bay's previous effort was the sort of once-in-a-lifetime masterpiece that somehow could appeal to the most superficial of viewers while also exploring erudite themes about the meaning of life, almost any follow-up was bound to be a step down. The safest bet probably would have been to scurry back to familiar territory, do another film like *The Rock*, stay in that lane for a few more movies and take another risk when it wouldn't be as career damaging.

On the other hand, *Armageddon* was such a big hit that Bay's stock was at an all-time high. The time to take a risk was now. How big a risk? Try this on for size – when you really examine it, *Pearl Harbor* is essentially three movies. The only way Michael Bay could top the ambitiousness of his previous film was to forge a trilogy of films, all contained within the same movie.

The first "film" is a throwback love story set in the immediate pre-World War II era. Military pilots Rafe (Ben Affleck) and Danny (Josh Hartnett) have been lifelong friends, and now Rafe is going off to join a squadron of American pilots flying with the British. The Americans have yet to enter the war, but Rafe is eager to see combat. In flashback we see the beginning of his courtship with Army Nurse Evelyn, played by Kate Beckinsale. Tonally, it's not terribly dissimilar to the films produced in the era in which the movie is set. Rafe and Evelyn have a meet-cute when she gives Rafe his medical exam and is persuaded to pass him even though he can't read the eye chart. (He explains his problem is dyslexia, not poor vision.) This provokes a whirlwind courtship that truly is the first time Bay has dabbled in real romance, the brief A.J./Grace subplot in *Armageddon* notwithstanding.

While Rafe goes off to England, Danny, Evelyn and many of Evelyn's nurse friends are assigned to Pearl Harbor. Here the war is so distant that the peace enjoyed there doesn't even feel like the calm before the storm. Instead, one gets the sense that the storm might entirely bypass them. That changes when word comes in that Rafe was shot down and presumed dead. Danny and Evelyn first comfort each other, then avoid crossing paths for three months. When they do renew their acquaintance, they fall hard for each other almost as quickly and Rafe and Evelyn did. Even though they are both still in mourning, the affair is quickly consummated.

As it turns out, Rafe was not killed in action. Instead he was rescued from the water crash of his plane by a French fishing boat. It took him month to get back home – arriving on December 6, 1941 - and the truth about Evelyn and Danny's coupling doesn't stay hidden for long. Of course, this leads to conflict between the two former best friends.

This sets the stage for chapter 2 of the trilogy, which is the Japanese attack on Pearl Harbor that occurred on December 7. The preamble and assault on Pearl Harbor occupy about forty minutes of screentime, beginning with the ambush of Battleship Row and continuing as Rafe and Danny rally a few pilots to reach an airfield. They make it into the air and shoot down several Japanese planes, though it's a clear victory for the Japanese. Parallel to this, Evelyn and her friends work to save the hundreds of wounded, unfortunately having to triage and leave several men to die. Following the attack, President Roosevelt addresses Congress and asks them to declare a state of war with Japan.

This provokes the third chapter of the film, which is built around the American response to Pearl Harbor – Doolittle's raid. Rafe and Danny are part of a squadron of bombers that attacks Tokyo, doing only negligible damage, but serving to both boost American morale and make Japan nervous about how vulnerable they could be to an attack.

There's likely enough story in each chapter that would have allowed for expansion into its own feature length. Indeed, if one were to start their viewing at the point in the film where the Japanese approach Pearl Harbor, that tense build-up would more than suffice as an opening sequence. That's a rare observation to be able to make an hour and twenty minutes into the film. What helps this along is the fact that very little of that opening hour does much to illuminate the Japanese motivations for the attack.

In his review, Roger Ebert took the film to task for that omission, saying, "If you have the slightest knowledge of the events in the film, you will know more than it can tell you. There is no sense of history, strategy or context," noting that the Japanese motivations for the attack are unclear. Again, with respect to the frequently insightful Mr. Ebert, he takes it at face value that this omission is a mistake of some kind. One detail that is abundantly clear from the middle act Pearl Harbor sequence is that this is a film very embedded to the American experience at that time. Bay and his collaborators are not attempting to make a documentary of some sort, they're instead forming an emotional reality. This is why the film begins with such emphasis on that primal human emotion – love.

Bay addresses some of the "historical inconsistencies" in an essay on his website, reprinted from *Pearl Harbor – The Movie and the Moment*. A key passage explains, "As I got deeper and deeper into my research, I learned that historians have different views and theories about what happened at Pearl. The Pentagon, which worked closely with me on this movie, admitted that there was no real Navy or Army logs kept during this time period. And even the men and women who were actually in the attack have varying accounts of what happened."

If you questioned the average American on the evening of December 7, 1941 about why the Japanese did what they did, would they be able to answer at any length? Would there be any need for a motivation beyond the fact they were allied with Hitler, who was waging war across Europe? Perhaps more importantly, after having experienced the 40 minutes of screen time that encompasses the sneak attack, does the audience need the Japanese to have a motivation? The only fact that matters is that they ambushed a country they had no conflict with and thousands lost their lives brutally. The act would always demand retaliation, no matter the motivation, and do the dishonorable savages who carried out this attack deserve the dignity of a justification? Of course not.

A film need not show intense fidelity to the events it depicts, so long as the emotion it stirs is authentic to those provoked by real events. Michael Bay films are not about logic and plausibility; they are about the reactions those films provoke.

This reading becomes clearer once you understand the purpose of the film's third chapter. The Doolittle Raid is a military operation – conceived by Lt. Colonel James Doolittle (Alec Baldwin) - with comparatively little strategic benefit, save for allowing the American forces to do a little saber rattling. A cold, logical mind might not have deemed the operation worth the risk, but what's one emotion that can override that logic? Revenge!

The middle portion of *Pearl Harbor* is akin to the brutal rapes and murders in *The Last House on the Left* and films of its ilk. The audience is subjected to a violent, ugly, unjustifiable action for the purpose of dehumanizing the perpetrators in the same manner in which they did to their victims. Metaphorically, the bombing of Pearl Harbor is the rape, and the Doolittle Raid is where America goes all *Death Wish* on the Japanese. Nobody rapes the United States of America on Ben Affleck and Alec Baldwin's watch!

That third act is the cathartic release that all revenge films coast on. The trick is that these films work best with vile, unrepentant villains. Bay's motivation to obscure the Japanese motivations is understandable, but would have paid better dividends if he could have done a rewrite on history and had the Nazis attack Pearl Harbor. Nazis are the ultimate bad guys, the scum you can drop in any movie and walk away assured they will never, ever gain the sympathies of your audience. They're the black-hat evil that makes an audience blood-thirsty. Since the film can't play that particular card, the Doolittle Raid finds its adrenaline diminished somewhat.

This also forces the film to make sure the second act ratchets up the Japanese to as villainous levels as is allowed. One sequence that reportedly enraged the Japanese viewers and Pearl Harbor survivors alike was the attack on the hospital. In real life, the Japanese limited their attack to military targets, not civilians, under their misguided idea that made a sneak attack somehow more "honorable." To remain true to that might have afforded the enemy a dignity it did not deserve, and certainly would have robbed the film of the emotional gut punch the original attack carried. The completely fictional attack serves that purpose, for there should be no debate as to who the villains here are.

(Perhaps accidentally, this also echoes the black-and-white tone of the war films of the era as well as the inherent xenophobia that propaganda of that day was designed to evoke. One should not get incensed on Japan's part for their depiction here. The film is not depicting the modern Japan, but the Japan that existed in popular culture and warlike deed in that era.)

Bay proves himself more than capable of exaggerating for emotional truth in one of the film's best scenes, and one of the most transcendent moments of cinema. A jaw-dropping moment occurs when President Franklin Delino Roosevelt assembles his cabinet and orders them to formulate some sort of counter-strike against "the heart of Japan the way they hit us" in order to allow them to boost American morale. His advisors are skeptical, saying that "It can't be done."

At that point, the wheelchair-bound Commander-in-Chief muses that God must have put him in that chair for a reason. By manner of demonstration, he pushes back from the table, and then, in a halting fashion, pulls one foot out and grasps the table for support in getting to his feet. Others rush to his aide, but he orders them all back.

And then, in one of the most glorious moments of American cinema – FDR stands tall. The room hushed, he pronounces, "Do not tell me it can't be done."

Was FDR even capable of such a feat? It doesn't matter. All that matters is that through this moment, we feel his conviction as well as the belief in the impossible that surely coursed through anyone who supported FDR's seemingly difficult plan in real life. *Pearl Harbor* gains greater emotional authenticity the further it estranges itself from the actual events or even reasonable plausibility.

The only failing with Bay's approach is that he does not go far enough for maximum payoff. Once he has altered the events of the attack to that degree, it really should be no different to replace the Japanese with the Nazis. Then the third act could be a more climactic revenge against Germany.

The restrained approach would be to restage Doolittle's Raid above Germany, but as obvious as it is, the correct climax would be to drop atomic bombs on the Third Reich, utterly incinerating Hitler and the Nazis in a manner that would make the climax of *Raiders of the Lost Ark* look like a Mickey Mouse cartoon.

Perhaps it's on the nose, but sometimes that can be the only correct solution.

If Bay pulled back out of fear of alienating his audience, he surely kicked himself several years later when Quentin Tarantino released *Inglourious Basterds*, which featured Hitler being killed in a burning, exploding movie theatre. That blatant departure from history surely did not hurt the film's critical acclaim (89% on Rotten Tomatoes), nor its award appeal (eight Academy Award nominations.) It was Bay's mistake to be too conservative here.

The reason why there's so much preamble to the horrors of war is so that the audience can be fully rooted in the innocence of the time. We can see Bay adjusting his style throughout the film as a way of replicating the visual grammar of the films of the 40s. Those old movies are the connection the present has with that era. If 1941 was shot like *The Rock*, it would somehow feel unnatural and perhaps "too modern" for film audiences. Bay doesn't totally crank his style back to that era of filmmaking, but he restrains his love for quick cuts and fast camera movements. The result is a movie that looks merely conventional in a great many moments, but for Bay, it must have been like trying to swim through Jello.

Both stylistically and from a story standpoint, the first third of the film presents considerable risk. The sequence that introduces the adult Rafe and Danny allows Bay to indulge in some hot shot flying sequences, but from that point on, the focus is squarely on the characters for longer than has ever happened in a Bay movie to this point.

But why romance? The answer can be summed up in one word: *Titanic*.

On the *Armageddon* commentary, Bay erroneously recalled how *Titanic* influenced the development of the love story in *Armageddon*. It's possible he was actually thinking of the development of this project, which takes so many cues from *Titanic* that it's a wonder the Japanese mission wasn't about them trying to capture the "Heart of the Ocean" diamond. Both films are epic romances set against even more epic tragedies. Fictional characters are weaved in alongside famous players, and the movie even came with its radio-friendly ballad. (To be fair, *Armageddon* had one too.)

And in typical Bay fashion, he must have asked, "Why have just one romance when you can have two?" (This likely came on the heels of positing, "What kind of coward limits himself to just one epic historic event per movie?") The result is a love triangle that sputters because the Danny/Evelyn romance never feels as epic as the love between Rafe and Evelyn. The movie has already flat-out told us that Rafe and Evelyn's love is the "most romantic" ever. Danny is barely developed before Rafe disappears and only gets a little bit of space to make his mark during Rafe's absence. Hartnett obliges by making no effort to leave a strong impression with his performance.

If Affleck was the intended lead of the film, the entire enterprise would have been royally screwed by the fact that he vanishes for nearly a complete half-hour while the film attempts to convince us he's dead. It's a good thing that Beckinsale is the star because—wait, what? She's NOT the star? But then why does she have the most important leg in the love triangle? By making the first hour and twenty minutes centered on a love triangle between two men and a woman, Bay has directly made the female the most critical role in that triangle. She's the only one who can make a choice that the whole movie turns on. Both men are subject to her whims.

Affleck's supposed to be the lead? Are you really sure about that?

Okay, let's talk about Affleck here for a little bit. There's a definite sense that Bay is trying to repeat here his role in making Will Smith an icon. In *Bad Boys*, Bay took the first step in redefining the Fresh Prince only to see another director snatch him up and complete the transformation with his next project. It only makes sense that after priming the Affleck pump on *Armageddon*, Bay would call dibs on the follow-through.

On Bay's last two films, the casts were headed by icons of masculinity – Sean Connery and Bruce Willis. Bay didn't have to make stars so much as exploit them. *Pearl Harbor* is the first time since *Bad Boys* that he doesn't have an iconic actor in one of his lead roles. This is entirely a self-starting cast, with all of the A-listers (and let's be honest, former A-listers) buried in the supporting roles. If you want to know why true stars get a lot of money, examine the difference between *Pearl Harbor* and the two movies that came before it.

Affleck's not really to blame here. This could have been his Will-Smith-in-*Independence-Day* but his long absence from the story really cuts into that. Danny is present throughout the entire picture, though, so maybe he'd have carried the film better from that vantage. After all, Danny gets Evelyn pregnant and he also… hmm… I'm sure he does something significant. Ah yes! He's one of the few pilots to get into the air at Pearl Harbor, though the Japanese lose only 29 planes total out of 350 and the battle ends because the Admiral orders a withdrawal. So… what else? He flies in Doolittle's raid, but his actions could have been performed by anyone. I guess his death is important because it allows Rafe to resume his romance with Evelyn.

So yeah, Danny's not really a great role.

Of course at this point, Affleck was still a bit shy of becoming an iconic actor. Even though he's playing a flyboy, he lacks the rogue qualities of a Harrison Ford or a Tom Cruise. I can't speak to the concept of him being a teenage girl dreamboat like Leonardo DiCaprio in *Titanic,* but then *Titanic* knew enough not to let Leo disappear from the screen for too long.

Armageddon managed to keep a lot of balls in the air and be a film that touched its audience in a wide variety of ways. Those viewers who wanted just to focus on the pretty visuals were able to do that and still get emotional fulfilment via the visuals, while those looking for deeper meaning were able to find it in those deeper layers. The key was having a strong core that all those satellites could orbit. Without that, the film has to ask more of its audience, always a risky prospect.

No one would accuse Bay of a lack of ambition on this film, but *Pearl Harbor* proves to be a more challenging film for both him and his audience because he both discards the traditional core of the story and denies himself some of his best magic tricks that connect him to his viewers.

Most students of Hollywood structure know that a significant turning point in the structure usually occurs around the 10-15 minute mark. In *Pearl Harbor*, that turning point comes not with a battle, but with the first meeting between Rafe and Evelyn. Right here, we're told "These are your heroes. This is where your attention should be. This is the story we are telling." Bay has a nifty way of dressing this encounter up, setting the meeting in the past and chopping the flashback up as Evelyn relates the tale to her friends.

With trademark subtlety, Bay has his actors even adopt the diction of those 40s romances. It's slight, but you can perceive a distinction between their cadence (and even their accents) in this sequence versus the rest of the film. They almost appear to be imitating actors in a Howard Hawks production. I can't say this with any authority, but I imagine Bay surely enjoyed the chance to pay homage to one of his influences.

What follows is a much-mocked scene where a broken-nosed Rafe attempts to charm Evelyn with a bottle of champagne. A miscalculation while opening it sends the cork right into his nose, leaving him in considerable pain. Is it silly? Perhaps, but it's an opportunity where Evelyn yet again has the upper hand in the relationship. As much as Rafe is presented as a square-jawed alpha male, Bay delights in taking the piss out of him and letting him be human.

(Uh-oh. We're in uncharted waters here. If there's one thing *The Rock* taught us it's that the every-man we laugh at is never the alpha male. But then again, Nicolas Cage did ultimately get to save the day in that film, so this isn't dire. Yet.)

Those who find the sequence corny are again overlooking that the movie itself tells us it's not. One of the nurses, Sandra (Jennifer Garner) says "That's the most romantic story I've ever heard." Evelyn herself says that it's been "the most romantic four weeks and twelve days of my life," while the other nurses get all moony-eyed and profess to be jealous of her. That should settle the matter for detractors of this sequence.

There's always concern and misunderstanding over how Bay handles women in his films, but again we are presented with a movie that challenges the party line on his female leads. It leads an audience to ponder, "Maybe this is on purpose. Have we been given a bait-and-switch where we only thought Rafe was our lead?"

Furthermore, throughout the movie, it is Evelyn who makes the most emotional impact. She has the most affecting emotional arc as she mourns Rafe when he's presumed dead. Later she not only has to deal with sleeping with his friend, but the emotional turmoil when Rafe turns up alive. In the film's second segment, her bravery – and that of the other nurses – nearly overshadows the battle. Rafe, Danny and the others are trained to deal with combat and in Rafe's case, have been itching for it. Evelyn and her colleagues not only have to perform under conditions they never expected, but it is they who are looking the men in the eye as they die, they who have to triage and determine who has a chance to live and who will be left to die. The men make the mess, but it's the women who have to mop it up.

Even in the third act, the film manages to find something for Evelyn to do as the action moves to the Tokyo bombing. She uses the kindness she showed one wounded soldier to call in a favor with him and be at the information hub as news of the raid comes in. It's a fairly small detail that could have easily been cut, but in showing us that this is a gross violation of regulations, it drives home how remarkable Evelyn is for pulling this off.

Is it going too far to say that Evelyn is one of Michael Bay's strongest protagonists, male or female? Is it absurd to show that through her treatment here, Bay reveals himself to be a pure feminist? I don't think so. Kate Beckinsale is considered one of the sexiest women alive, but is presented in an almost demure fashion here. And a second look at the geekier nurse of the group reveals her to be Jennifer Garner, not even a year ahead of becoming a major sex symbol on the television show *Alias*. The raw material is right there if Bay wanted to sex things up. Instead, he goes for romance, which may have disappointed the teenage boys in the audience, but surely won the hearts of teenage girls.

But this is the conflict inherent in *Pearl Harbor*. In attempting something outside his comfort zone, Bay risks the ire of those who attend his movies for the same things they've found in earlier films. An early-era Beatles fan who worships "Love Me Do" might not follow the group when they release something like "I Am the Walrus."

Don't scoff. There's every indication Bay did see this film as a departure in several respects. His first assistant director on the film, K.C. Holdenfield, recalled to *GQ* how Bay reported to set with a determination to make this film look different from his already-distinctive style. "The first day we started shooting, he wasn't using his fast-moving, fast cuts, low shots—his bag of tricks—and it was like watching an Italian speak without his hands. By lunchtime, we're making a Michael Bay movie, in the Michael Bay style."

With respect to Holdenfield, while the movie's style might not be restrained as aggressively as Bay set out, the pacing of the cuts feels slower than typical for the auteur. One need only to notice the propensity of longer shots in the December 7th setpiece to recognize this isn't the typical Michael Bay chop-chop-chop job. In the build-up to the attack, he very much favors slow, sweeping pans that give a sense of scope and wonderment. Some examples of this include:

- The long shot of the Japanese planes approaching the skies above Hawaii. It's just one long take as more planes overtake the camera, no cutting or beauty shots of individual planes in the fleet.
- A slow right-to-left pan that uses the perspective of some hiking boys to show the low-flying plans over a landscape.
- A similar and shorter shot going left-to-right as the planes soar over a baseball diamond.
- Several longer, wider shots that allow the planes to be seen in the background, yet unnoticed by the characters in the frame.

In between, there are shots of the principles and the stage-setting moments of those going about their duties on the ships, sleeping on their couches, and so on. It's a slower tempo, one that invites the audience to take in the entire mise-en-scene. The cuts accelerate at the top of the attack, but even then there's the sense that tension is built through the frame, not through manipulative editing. One sequence of a torpedo being dropped in the water is particularly effective, using only a POV of the torpedo and then cutting to outside the water as we watch it approach its target and impact.

Staging like this allows the audience to experience the attack as an observer on that day might have. True, the editing allows for many perspectives to be intercut, but there's an early effort to make the viewer feel more like they are present in the moment rather than being an omniscient observer. After the first impact, we cut to the perspectives of Rafe and Danny, who are some distance away and see the attack at that remove. Even during the chaos of the attack, Bay's love of extreme close-ups is curbed. With the scope widened, the full terror of the attack surrounds us, making the Japanese as overwhelming as they must have appeared on that morning. Bay knows how to stage a suspenseful build-up and payoff. This is no mere CGI orgy. His angles have been carefully chosen, frequently making us aware of either a target or an ordinance approaching that target, and then making the audience endure the unalterable seconds leading up to impact. The shots dealing with the bomb that cripples the *Arizona* are a good example of this. The overlong build-up makes the money shot of the ship buckling at the blast even more painful.

To recap the entire battle would take more space and effort than is necessary. Suffice to say that anyone who claims this is the "same old Michael Bay" hasn't watched the film closely. Even when dealing with material that's his bread and butter, he shoots it in a way largely unlike his previous action efforts. That he found a middle ground between his normal look and his original intentions maters not. When watching all of his films in sequence, you can see an evolution throughout them. The difference that for the first three films, the evolution is largely in one direction in terms of pacing. *Pearl Harbor* reverses that entirely, to the point where it might fit more as a middle-ground between *Bad Boys* and *The Rock*.

The Monkey's Paw of that deal is that since he's stripped of the visual shorthand that makes icons out of men, he's less able to compensate when directing mere mortals. If Bay was fully able to remold Affleck the way he did Smith in *Bad Boys*, the flyboy probably would have stood a better chance of being a sex symbol. When he can't go "full Bay" the actors have take up the slack. Ben Affleck is a fine actor, capable of great performances. (Just watch *Hollywoodland*. And he was the bomb in *Phantoms*, yo!) But he needs the Michael Bay hero cam. The same could be said for Kate Beckinsale. She gives a performance that would be fine for a scaled-down indie movie that really needs us to feel every nuance, but this movie is clearly calling for a goddess, a feminist icon. Try as she might, she's just not there yet.

It's hard to say if this was a case of Bay wanting more of an everyman feel to his film, or just a misunderstanding of how much lesser the performances become when his camera can't support them aggressively. I do think that this gave Bay determination to prove that he could make an icon out of someone with no pre-established screen image, just to show that he could have pulled it off here if he wanted to.

Pearl Harbor made about $100 million less worldwide than *Armageddon* did, but it was only a few million shy of its predecessor domestically. Considering the film's three-hour length and the American patriotism at its core, those numbers are pretty good.

However, critics were less kind to the film. Rotten Tomatoes puts *Armageddon* at 39% fresh while *Pearl Harbor* is at 25% fresh. I suspect that Bay himself believed the project fell short of his ambitions. He'd taken a risk and the critics seemed not to appreciate the courage that required. The fact that he himself might have been less satisfied with the result might have made those notices sting a little more this time. *Pearl Harbor* apparently began with the intentions of being a huge departure for Bay, but the half-measures he ended up with must have felt like a retreat and the attempt to top *Titanic*'s love story backfired.

My own feeling is that Bay made this movie as a vulnerable man. He consciously tried to be a different kind of filmmaker, and even if the critics didn't approve, he probably hoped they would at least notice. It's not hard to notice the conscious departures Bay makes here in his style so the negative reviews must have stung. I can think of few other reasons why he would have embarked on the subsequent projects he did.

While *Pearl Harbor* may not be a perfect film it should be noted for its feminist overtones and its revolutionary approach to emotional truth. Whether the film proves to be more than the sum of its parts is, of course, in the eye of the beholder. One overlooked value it provides is in illuminating those areas where Bay's regular approach would have elevated the film. Thus, through their absence, they teach us how potent his bag of tricks really is. *Pearl Harbor* may help you accept Bay as a visionary, if not on the merits of this film alone, what it teaches us about his entire filmography.

Bad Boys II (2003)

Release date: July 18, 2003
Story by Cormac Wibberley & Marianne Wibberley and Ron Shelton
Screenplay by Ron Shelton and Jerry Stahl
Produced by Jerry Bruckheimer
Budget: $130 million
Domestic box office: $138.6 million
Global box office: $273.3 million

Must I?

In every career, there are peaks and there are valleys. As we've discussed so far, all of Michael Bay's works up to this point have exhibited some virtues. Many of the movies have been quite well-crafted, with deep nuance and subtlety. Even when he's misstepped, as happened in portions of *Pearl Harbor*, it was in the service of attempting to scale greater heights and challenge his craft.

And then there's *Bad Boys II*, which represents such a severe backslide that it leads one to conclude that Bay was so dissatisfied with the results of *Pearl Harbor*, he retreated back to familiar territory like a scarred college freshman fleeing to the comfort of his parents' home on weekends. If that wasn't the motivation, then the only other possible ambition must be that Bay was so frustrated by how the first *Bad Boys* turned out that he resolved to return to that universe when he had the control to do it right.

The *Bad Boys* films were the only two Bay films I had never watched prior to embarking on this book. Because of this, the post-viewing reflects for those films were more complicated than for the movies I was merely revisiting. I have to admit that I struggled to put this film in some sort of artistic context. The conclusions that came so naturally when peeling back the layers in the other films were frustratingly denied to me here. I eventually decided that while Bay must have been lured to the project by the concept of doing the first film "right," he quickly fell out of love with it.

Tom Hanks's directing debut was a 1996 film called *That Thing You Do*, centering on a fictional one-hit wonder rock band called The Wonders in 1964. On the eve of the band's appearance at a local talent show, their drummer is injured and Guy Patterson (Tom Everett Scott) steps in to keep time on their song "That Thing You Do." It's a slow-tempo love ballad but when the band takes the stage, a bored Guy cranks the speed up to amuse himself. Though the band is initially thrown, they quickly catch up and more importantly, the crowd loves it! No longer a sappy love song, the number becomes rock and roll!

Basically, *that* is what Michael Bay is doing throughout *Bad Boys II*, compensating for a weak script by cranking everything up to be bigger and showier. The deficiency here is that he's not riding on a strong melody. "That Thing You Do" has a catchy tune that is only enhanced by being up-tempo. Without the music, all you'd have is a fast drumbeat.

Bad Boys II is a fast pounding of the drums being made by Michael Bay to keep himself amused because if the whole ship is going down at least he should have some fun, right?

The stakes in the three previous Bay films were much higher. In *The Rock*, an entire city was at risk. In *Armageddon*, all of human civilization was on the line, and in *Pearl Harbor*, the very concept of freedom was threatened. And then in *Bad Boys II,* the cops are trying to stop a drug dealer.

This is not to say that the fate of the world has to be threatened in order for a film to work. However, three straight films have shown that Bay's bombastic style works best when the threat is equally overblown and direct. Here the stakes are smaller and the plot is meandering.

The basic story has the two detectives hunting the source of ecstasy that's coming into Miami. Mike Lowrey (Will Smith) and Marcus Burnett (Martin Lawrence) have little luck early on hunting the distributor. Neither one is initially aware that Marcus's sister Syd (Gabrielle Union) is actually a DEA agent working the same case while undercover as a money launderer for the Russian Mob. The Russians are in a deal with the Cuban drug lord Tapia - the Cubans make the drug and the Russians sell it in their Miami nightclubs. Beyond this set-up, the plot isn't really worth recapping in extensive detail. At the end of Act Two, Syd's cover is blown and she's taken back to Cuba as a prisoner of the cartel. Members of the Miami SWAT team and Syd's comrades in the DEA team up for an off-the-books mission to get her back.

The film quickly becomes one of those "and this happened, and then this happened, and then this happened" movies. I saw these a lot during my time as a script reader. It was always hard to stay invested in these scripts because even if the goal was clearly defined, an overcomplicated plot becomes a chore to keep up with because it's not complex so much as it is crowded. More than any other Bay film, the plot feels like it exists only to fill in the gaps between the set-pieces. It's "plot-caulk."

If you sat Bay down and invited him to explain how the story moves from A to B to C, I'm not sure that he could tell you. With the added complication of the Haitian mob, the film has three major bad guy players on the board, plus the Miami PD/DEA conflict and yet it still finds time for domestic silliness with Marcus's family. It's enough to make you long for the cliché of the loner cop just so you won't have to sit through scenes of an over-protective Marcus threatening a man there to take his daughter on a date.

This film is a loud, kinetically edited and shot, pretty picture with a story that finds itself a low priority. Bay knows how to handle the action well. There are two well-choreographed sequences of car chase mayhem in Miami, plus a great raid on the Cuban mansion and a car chase that follows. It's almost as if Bay decided to give the critics the film they swore they'd been seeing from him for years.

Unlike the first film, this feels like a Bay vehicle through and through. This is oddly jarring, as disconcerting as if Leonardo DiCaprio returned to TV for a revival of *Growing Pains*. The only element that has possibly grown more than Bay himself is the budget. Though the first one was made for a tight $19 million, the sequel reportedly cost $130 million. As the action sequences are among the film's few highlights, they definitely got bang for their buck. On the other hand, after recording *The White Album,* the Beatles didn't decide to revisit and rerecord *Meet the Beatles* so perhaps it would have been best for Bay not to look back once he and his lead actors had outgrown their place here.

Almost nothing about the look of the sequel resembles the original movie. Bay's Miami is photographed with a lot of hot oranges and cool blues, a style that becomes more prevalent in Bay vehicles going forward (and perhaps not coincidentally, also emerges in Tony Scott's films of that era as well.) The look and feel of the picture oddly has more in common with *2 Fast 2 Furious,* which was released the same year and also was filmed and set in Miami. Had both films been made in the era of franchise crossovers, perhaps they could have just made *Bad Boys 2 Fast 2 Furious* and only subjected audiences to one film rather than two. (A feature film adaptation of Will Smith's hip-hop hit "Miami" might also have been preferable.)

The relatively conservative camera work of the first film is replaced by Bay's frequently moving, camera shots. It's as if every tool he denied himself excess usage of in *Pearl Harbor* is now let off the leash and cranked all the way up. Bay dives into his old vices like a formerly pregnant woman now free to nosh on as much sushi and lunchmeat as she desires, to say nothing of the alcohol she can freely chase it with.

Just look at the slow-motion reveal of Will Smith's Mike Lowrey, flinging off his disguise of a Klansman's robe in slow-motion, arms outstretched in opposite directions with a gun in each hand. It's a glorious, giddy over-the-top moment that evokes a superhero transformation. Will Smith is so much the action hero that this moment boarders on parody.

What helps a little is that Will Smith is in full "Big Willie Style" mode. This film arrived in the middle of a decade-long period where Will Smith ruled the world with such hits as *Independence Day*, *Men in Black* and *Enemy of the State*. The star's natural charisma and confidence are in full-force here. You could be forgiven if the Will Smith of the first film didn't quite strike you as a fully-fledged movie star, but he's larger than life in this outing. Bay uses it to good effect, but fails to amp up the bad guys to compensate. Smith blows everyone else off the screen in a competition that resembles Superman vs. Steven Hawking in a one-on-one game of "Horse."

This swamp confrontation is hardly the only big moment in the film, or even in this sequence. Before this run-in with the KKK is over, we'll have followed a bullet in slow-motion as it heads towards impact. It's a big showy, "look at me! I'm directing!" moment, but it's rather thrown away on what proves to be a minor scene from a story standpoint. In most films, that's the kind of razzle-dazzle that would be held back for an edge-of-your-seat moment in the climax. For Bay, it's just another day at the office.

Slightly more effective, but no less showy is a sequence later in the film that finds Lowrey and Burnett in a room in a shootout with criminals on the opposite side of the wall. Rather than cut back and forth, Bay stages the action in a way that makes it appear as if the two rooms are on a turntable, being spun past the camera in time with each side's dialogue exchanges. It's the sort of move that Hitchcock or Tarantino might have used for one revolution. Bay uses it for just over two full spins the first time, and three full spins the second time. A couple more times and he'd almost rival the number of revolutions made by the *Wheel of Fortune* in an average week.

The film also includes perhaps the most infamous of Bay's signature moves. At the end of the second act, Marcus's sister has been kidnapped and he gets a phone call from the bad guys giving their terms if he ever wants to see her alive again. In this incredibly iconic shot, Marcus rises up into frame in slow-motion as the camera spins around him. His face hardens as Mike also rises into the shot. The camera cuts closer, to being another spin around Marcus, who says, "Shit just got real." It's such a defining moment that it was used in Edgar Wright's *Hot Fuzz* as a later launching pad for over-the-top parody of action film excess. When the lights dim for Michael Bay's Lifetime Achievement clip reel at the Academy Awards, you can bet that moment will be part of it.

If you've read this far into the book, you'll recognize I've defended (or perhaps more accurately, justified) Bay's stylistic excess in the earlier entries. That's because in the past, Bay's visual pyrotechnics have usually been in service of a strong story or an impactful theme. Here, one can't help but sense that Bay is… overcompensating.

As big as Bay goes, one can't escape the feeling that he's trapped in a genre he's outgrown. The buddy-cop film can only become so large before it steps into self-parody. If Bay was riding on a script like *21 Jump Street,* that might have actually worked, particularly considering the comedic chops of the performers. After the outsize nature of previous Bay releases, seeing him struggle within the confines of this world is a little like seeing Lady Gaga bring her stadium-sized bombast into a tiny coffee house.

If *Pearl Harbor* felt long in places, it was because it was dealing with tremendous scope and was clearly trying to tell three distinct stories. *Bad Boys II* doesn't have that excuse and if it was willing to lose a few scenes to get the running time down to two hours, the removal of those detours might have brought some clarity. In particular, a long sequence where Mike and Marcus give the third degree to a teenager who arrives to pick Marcus's daughter up for a date seems to have snuck in from another movie. Back when *Anchorman* was made, those filmmakers actually shot an entire subplot that was never used. This sub-story amounted to so much screen time that the filmmakers were able to marry it with other alternate takes and release it straight to DVD under the title *Wake Up, Ron Burgundy: The Lost Movie.* Pretty much every moment in *Bad Boys II* dealing with Marcus's family drama feels like a stray scene from the *Bad Boys II* equivalent of *Wake Up, Ron Burgundy* that accidently was left in the final master when the film prints were made.

Another particularly distasteful moment comes during one of the car chases, where Mike and Marcus pursue a morgue van being used by the bad guys. In sickening fashion, several cadavers tumble out of the van and onto the street mid-chase, leaving our heroes no choice but to drive over them. It's a rather morbid moment that seems unsure if it should be horrifying or funny. (The actors seem to be playing it as comedy, which doesn't help.) This eventually lays the groundwork for the discovery that the bad guys are smuggling drugs and money via the corpses, but that's a pretty unpleasant path to take to get to that revelation.

The main area where the script falls short is that it doesn't give the lead characters very strong arcs. The first shootout introduces the idea of some tension between Mike and Marcus that has Marcus rethinking their partnership. The only problem with this is that it mostly manifests by having the two of them bicker like an old married couple. Since that's the way they *always* bicker, the film runs into trouble conveying that this is a more serious split between them. Marcus's discomfort with Mike dating his sister falls under the same category. It plays as sitcom-level big brother over-protectiveness, not an actual betrayal between the two. It would be easy to lay the blame on the two sitcom actors for playing the material wrong, but the fact is the storyline and the dialogue do a poor job of conveying any growth or tension between the two. That's one emotion that's a lot harder to manufacture with a few camera tricks. Bay might be able to shoot his heroes as if they're demigods, but that bombast renders moot any attempt to use creative staging and blocking to subtly communicate the inter-character conflict.

Were the critics right all along? I tend to look it as a "stopped clock is right twice a day" sort of thing. The fact that they're right about this film in no way lends weight to any shots they might have taken against Bay's earlier films. It's not so much that the Emperor is naked as it is that he packed entirely the wrong wardrobe for this outing.

    Among the film's few virtues is that it's largely post-racial. Even some eleven years later it's all too rare to see a mainstream broad-appeal film where all three lead actors are African-American. Even more remarkable is that race is rarely remarked upon within the film. The KKK scene is the most obvious exception, but putting that aside and a few lines here and there, the film might as well be color-blind.

    Sadly, this is the film where I have to note that the stereotypical "Michael Bay women" show up in force. The club and beach scenes make for more conspicuous placement of the curvy model/stripper types that Bay seems to favor. After films where the timeframe or the settings presented obstacles to that kind of indulgence, Bay cuts loose here. We could argue that the presence of Syd as a forceful lead character somewhat negates that, but then, the movie finds plenty of time to get her into a bikini, short skirts and the third act revolves around her needing to be rescued.

    Behind the scenes, this film is also remembered as the final theatrical collaboration between Bay and Jerry Bruckheimer. In this, their fifth film, there's a sense that Bay has come full circle by returning to the series that launched his career. I'd like to think that Bay realized he was stagnating and that the experience of trying to re-freshen old ground convinced him it was time to make a drastic change. Perhaps he and Bruckheimer had become like a marriage that needed to end, or maybe it was as simple as Bay feeling like he was ready to "graduate." Like Luke Skywalker looking up into the skies and seeking adventure, perhaps Bay was just ready to blaze his own path independent of the Bruckheimer legacy.

Though *Pearl Harbor* fell short of being a home run, its ambition at least ensured a few base hits. *Bad Boys II* seems not to put in the effort where it would truly make a difference. Thus, it remains Bay's first true misstep, while simultaneously being a monument to everything critics despise about the man's work. If you're a fan of *Armageddon* and you want to get a sense of how those scholarly types see Michael Bay, watch this movie. There aren't any grand ambitions or transcendent themes to get in your way here.

The Island (2005)

Release date: July 22, 2005
Story by Caspian Tredwell-Owen
Screenplay by Caspian Tredwell-Owen and Alex Kurtzman & Roberto Orci
Produced by Michael Bay, Ian Bryce, Walter F. Parkes
Budget: $126 million
Domestic box office: $35.8 million
Global box office: $127.1 million

"I personally think we have huge marketing challenges on this movie... I think ultimately it will hurt the movie, because I don't think a lot of people will find [it]."

So said Michael Bay to MTV during the week of *The Island's* debut in the summer of 2005. It was a frustrating situation for him because he was certain that the film worked for the audience that saw it. "I've heard so many people say, 'God, I never heard about this movie,' and then in the next sentence they'll say, 'I love this movie,' or 'I've never liked your movies, but I love this movie,'" he explained. For a filmmaker who always considered what the audience wanted or would enjoy to be one of the most important aspects of his films, this had to be frustrating.

After the creative backslide that was *Bad Boys II*, Bay surely was looking for a project that would be more of an intellectual challenge. Indeed, if he was as bored on *Bad Boys II* as this writer believes, it would make sense for him to shake things up by working with a new creative partner. Few directors would have a hard time saying no to a request when it came personally from Steven Spielberg, and in an interview with Blackfilm, Bay downplayed that any rift with Bruckheimer existed, saying that the two actually spoke on the phone when rumors spread he was considering directing the film. As he concluded the call, Bruckheimer took the opportunity to let Bay know that his office had passed on the script.

To date, Bay has yet to collaborate with Bruckheimer on a film again, despite making five films after *The Island*. (In fairness, four of those are *Transformers* films, which Bruckheimer's deal with another studio would have precluded him from being involved with anyway.) In the same conversation, he explained why the siren song from DreamWorks was too seductive to turn a deaf ear to. "It's a more intimate studio," he said. "They're very supportive. DreamWorks is very supportive of making the script right. They gave me a lot of free rein."

With the knowledge that Bay was given great autonomy in resculpting the script, it becomes not unreasonable to ascribe a number of the themes and messages of the film to his own philosophy. When *The Island* is examined in context with his concurrent filmic output, the state of some of his business relationships, and the general tenor of the film industry, it's not hard to see some very pointed criticisms of the film industry.

The early segments of *The Island* are set in a contained underground compound where the residents' habits and meals are carefully monitored and regimented. Supposedly, they must all live this way because the outside world is too contaminated to support life, save for one island. Limited space means that residents can only move from the compound to the island if they win a weekly lottery. Lincoln Six Echo (played by Ewan McGregor) has been an inhabitant of the compound for three years, and is confused by strange dreams he has of a boat that don't seem to come from his own memories. This concerns Dr. Merrick, one of the colony leaders, who is keeping an unusually close watch on Lincoln.

All of this feels like standard dystopian fare, with a small dash of Hitchcockian paranoia thrown in. Before long, Lincoln learns the truth about the lottery. It's all a pretense to remove residents from the colony so that they can be harvested for organs and then killed. Lincoln secretly witnesses a woman who gives birth and then is killed by her doctors. The viewer then witnesses the nurse take the baby away… to the waiting arms of a mother who looks exactly like the birth mother. The dirty secret of the community is that everyone there is a clone, bred from the DNA of their sponsors so that they could be used as genetic donors and surrogates.

Now aware that "winning" the lottery is a death sentence, Lincoln rushes to help his friend Jordan Two Delta (Scarlett Johansson), who was just named this week's winner. The two manage to escape into the outside world and track down a colony worker whom Lincoln befriended. This worker manages to spell out the truth for the child-like and naïve clones, and point them in the direction of Lincoln's sponsor before he's killed by a mercenary hired to bring back the fugitives.

There are a lot of echoes of earlier dystopian sci-fi films, including *Logan's Run* and *THX-1138*, and indeed, by 2005 a sci-fi film was hardly breaking new ground by exploring the morality of human cloning. *The Island* certainly raises many questions that provided fodder for other films, such as if clones should be considered sentient autonomous people with right, or if they are little more than organ banks. Within the film, Dr. Merrick has led his customers to believe that the clones are kept in a persistent vegetative state and are not truly "alive" in the sense that one would think of any sentient being. The ethics of that are troubling enough, but the problematic questions that eugenics raises become even more aggressive when the clones are allowed to grow and evolve into distinct people of their own.

Should Lincoln's "sponsor" Tom Lincoln have the right to decide Lincoln Six Echo's fate? Is it moral for him to pay for the creation of a being who will be used merely to replenish his own organs? To what extent does Tom own his own DNA? These questions eventually lead to ones that parallel the abortion debate: When is something considered "alive?" When is it morally permissible to terminate that life? This is especially relevant to the conflict between Tom's ownership of his own DNA versus Lincoln Six Echo's own right to live. It's not hard at all to see the relationship between the moral qualms some have with abortion and similar concerns about stem-cell research and cloning.

But these are questions very near the surface of the film's context. Bay's themes are generally more deeply buried in the story so as to require greater effort to discover and excavate them. It should never be simple to find the true meaning of a Michael Bay film.

Without diminishing the depth to be found in those more surface-level questions, it's apparent to the seasoned Michael Bay aficionado that *The Island* is actually a metaphor for the creative process. Specifically, it is the Hollywood creative process of cloning old ideas and harvesting them to keep careers and franchises alive that is being taken to task here. This is a movie Michael Bay could only have made after the experience of making a sequel. It's both an expression of the frustration an artist feels as a prisoner of the system and also a defense of how that is the kind of life a creator needs to embrace in order for it to work.

If this seems far-fetched, it might help to remember that between *Bad Boys II* and *The Island*, Bay also produced two films through his company Platinum Dunes: *The Texas Chainsaw Massacre* and *The Amityville Horror*. Aside from being horror films, there's one other commonality the projects share – they're both remakes of pre-existing properties, clones, if you will. (In the interval between *The Island* and his next directing effort, *Transformers*, Bay would produce two more films – the prequel *Texas Chainsaw Massacre: The Beginning* and the remake *The Hitcher*.)

In that same MTV interview to promote the film, Bay discussed a very specific frustration with the business, "You see, what's going on in the studio system … we're making reruns of bad

TV shows now," he said. "I've got to tell you — it's really frustrating that there aren't a lot of fresh ideas out there." Though Bay never connected this idea to the themes of his film, it seems unlikely to be mere coincidence that this was on his mind while promoting it.

Hollywood had long had a love affair with sequels, but this period of time is where that affection became dominant to a degree not seen before. Studios sought to minimize their risk by putting their chips on established properties with brand recognition. This meant not only sequels, but remakes, reboots, prequels and adaptations from books and comic books. The logic went that existing properties came with pre-awareness and (hopefully) a built-in audience.

While this is appealing for studio underlings trying to dodge blame for backing a project that ends up having no commercial appeal, it is incredibly frustrating to directors who desperately have passion projects they wish to make. Even Martin Scorsese would probably have an easier time getting a film funded if it was based off of an existing I.P. (Intellectual Property) than he would a completely original screenplay. Bay was not immune to this frustration, speaking years later to *The Huffington Post* on the occasion of the release of *Pain & Gain*. "Studios just don't want to do this stuff now. They just want to do these big, big movies or they want to do these tiny little micro-movies. I mean, this is a $25 million movie," he said of the smaller project it took years to get off the ground.

Examining the film in this light lends new meaning to the cloning of people as it represents the cloning of franchises and properties. This connection is not as tenuous as it first appears once you examine the clues closely. Note that the clones are often referred to as an "Insurance Policy." Insurance Policy = I.P. = Intellectual Property. It also appears to be no accident that the clones are often referenced as "product lines." Within the film, this represents the dehumanizing and objectifying of the sentient beings as a way to justify their treatment. It also represents a subtle clue to the more subliminal themes that Bay has planted.

This may also be reinforced by the truly large number of product placements in the compound. This include: Puma sneakers, Speedo bathing suits, Xbox games, and Aquafina, all with prominently displayed logos. Thus the clones aren't just metaphorical stand-ins for brands, they are also immersed in them.

In the second half of the film, Lincoln Six Echo encounters his genetic sponsor, Tom. Though Tom is initially stunned to find out that his insurance policy is alive and has a mind of his own, he presents himself as an ally. Tom bought his insurance policy because he had been diagnosed with cirrhotic hepatitis and his liver would begin failing sometime in the next few years. He wanted to make sure there would be a compatible donor organ.

Lincoln asks Tom to help them expose what the Merrick Institute does, but exposure would mean Tom couldn't make use of his policy. Acting in his own interests, Tom secretly calls the Institute and tips them off, then betrays his clone. Following a car chase, the two men are discovered by the mercenaries as they fight in an abandoned building. Lincoln cleverly pretends to be Tom, even imitating his Scottish accent, and tricks the mercenaries into killing Tom instead. The duplicate has brought about the ruination of the original.

In examining what this means metaphorically, one ponders the duality it represents. As Lincoln is the sympathetic protagonist, it would be easy to assume that he represents Michael Bay (or any creator) in this parable on the creative process. I don't think it's that simple though. My read is that Bay is represented in the film by both Tom *and* Dr. Merrick. Tom's betrayal of Lincoln feels monstrous in the context of the film, but that's only because we have been manipulated to be on Lincoln's side from frame one. True, from a certain point of view, Tom is exploiting the clones, but only out of his own self-preservation. If Tom doesn't betray Lincoln, there's a very good chance he could die when his liver fails. Can we fault a man for doing whatever it takes to survive?

The translation of this theme would be: can we really hate the director for his hand in a remake (or clone) if that's the only way he can continue to work? Survival in Hollywood often means accepting that existing I.P. is one of the dominant forces in the industry. Should we blame Bay for producing the *Amityville* and *Texas Chainsaw* remakes? He's not the guy who funded them, he's just the guy who was trying to make a living by delivering something that someone else was willing to pay for.

Dr. Merrick stands for a further progression of this ideal. Through Merrick is fully aware of what he's doing, he doesn't care because he focuses on the fact that his clients want the product. The ethics of his position are murkier because if he were to stop providing this service, the moral dilemma he and his clients face would cease to exist. Thus, if Dr. Merrick represents Bay, it produces a reading that producers and directors like Bay are significantly culpable for the Hollywood prominence of existing I.P. exploitation. If directors stopped taking assignments on remakes, perhaps this trend would cease to be financially viable and audiences would rediscover new ideas of out necessity.

Lincoln represents that existing I.P., that *Texas Chainsaw Massacre* project which asks its creatives, "Why? Why must you recreate me? Why must you butcher and exploit me for your own ends?" It wouldn't surprise me if Bay is kept up at night wrestling with the question of who he truly is: Tom, the guy just trying to survive, or Merrick, the jackal profiting from exploitation? If all Bay wants to do is continue creating, is he evil if the only avenue open to him is replication?

To come at this element of the film from a slightly different angle, the Tom/Lincoln confrontation is interesting because one reading of it suggests we should not pity the original who has willfully exploited his own property. Indeed, Tom is "punished" for his exploitation when his clone turns against him and outlives him. Is the message that the risk of making derivative art is that it devalues the original? In this case, it certainly allows the copy to supplant the original entirely.

That is always the risk with remakes. If your *Psycho* remake is terrible enough, it could tarnish the brand entirely, bring crass commercialism to what was previously singular and unique. To put it another way, there's likely an entire generation that knows The Who's classic song "Behind Blue Eyes" through its horribly-rendered Limp Bizkit rendition. (And don't even get me started on sampling. I'll burn a whole chapter talking about the horrors that P. Diddy and Jessica Simpson inflicted on The Police and John Mellencamp, respectively.) A close study of Bay's oeuvre reveals him to be a champion of original ideas so the barely-concealed assault on the crass commercialism of the industry shown here should come as little surprise.

Earlier I mentioned that the film avails itself of certain themes and aesthetics that have existed in dystopian fiction for some time now. This similarity is also clearly no accident. If the start of the film feels derivative, that's intentional. How could a film with a sharp point of view about cloning *not* be deliberately evocative of earlier films? By introducing the world to us in this way, the film primes us to decode the themes of the picture related to the repugnance of remakes and reboots. A bit meta, perhaps, but Bay is wise to show restraint here rather than throw his own cleverness in our faces. When films like *Scream* display self-awareness, they are never content to just let that stand on its own. They always have to loudly announce that they are in on the joke. Bay's subtlety represents either faith in the intelligence of his audience, or security in the notion that his meaning is being communicated clearly.

The look and feel of the first portion of the film is another of those rare instances where Bay's direction is markedly reserved. The camera moves are slower and individual shots are allowed to linger longer. The color scheme and the high-contrast style that Bay favors is naturally in evidence, but the pace is far more moderated. We are drawn into Lincoln's world, made to experience the monotony he experiences. Within the Institute, Bay creates a world far unlike one he's shown us before.

Note that once the characters escape the confines of this "derivative" sci-fi world, it's akin to Dorothy arriving in Oz. Both they and we find ourselves in a whole new world. They barely have time to get their bearings before they end up in two massive chases on top of each other. The first hour of the film indulges in some chase scenes within the compound when Lincoln discovers the truth and later when he and Jordan escape. However, those moments are nothing when compared with the chase in a car followed by a jet bike pursuit. Then Bay tops all of that off by having his characters hang on a giant logo atop a skyscraper before it plummets to the ground. For a brief section of the picture, things turn into a pure Michael Bay action movie. It's a gear shift that carries far more impact because of how conservative the movie has been up to that point. It's a masterful manipulation of tone and pace that demonstrates the critics are wrong when they claim Bay makes every shot a money shot, pacing every 30-seconds of his films as if they were trailers or commercials.

This is Michael Bay's escape from the conventional. While he would not consider this the first film where he stretched himself, he surely knew the superficial critics would see it that way. Note the positive reviews for parts of this film. Roger Ebert gave it three stars, saying "The first half of Michael Bay's new film is a spare, creepy science fiction parable, and then it shifts into a high-tech action picture. Both halves work. Whether they work together is a good question. The more you like one, the less you may like the other. I liked them both, up to a point." In a 2014 examination of all of Bay's films, Indiewire said of *The Island* that it "may well be the most interesting film he's made so far." While overall critical reaction to the film was mixed, it seems that at least on some level, Bay had finally broken free of his critics' narrow perceptions, just as Lincoln and Jordan do.

Yet in the end, even after being put in a position where he could assume Tom's life easily, Lincoln goes back to the Institute so that he can free the other clones from the fate to which they've been condemned. In examining the third act, one might conclude that this film isn't just about Bay stretching himself. This is about Bay possibly sacrificing himself – his career, via the risks of this film - to burn down the system. If he can destroy the machine that holds them all captive, it would free all artists from their prisons. The end to cloning would mean a new beginning for original ideas. And truly, can you think of a better martyr for artistic integrity than Michael Bay?

This film represents another interesting milestone in Michael Bay's treatment of women. In an interesting wrinkle, all of the clones are raised in an unerotic environment, with their sexual development stalled at a pre-adolescent stage. (There's logic behind this as they certainly wouldn't want the clones to be breeding on their own.) In the colony we may see a few extras clothed in bathing suits, but the film doesn't linger on them, and certainly not in a leering way. It's impossible not to notice that many of the incidental women are model-beautiful, but that could just be commentary of the affluence behind the operation. Nothing shown on screen crosses the line into exploitation or eroticism.

Scarlett Johansson's Jordan is a woman who's treated exactly as the men are treated while within the colony, but once she and Lincoln get to the outside world, *that* is when the film makes a point of drawing attention to her beauty. Tom comments on having seen her in "men's magazines" then has a conversation with Lincoln that's dripping with his lust and objectification towards her. The only thing he might find more remarkable than her physical beauty is the fact that Lincoln hasn't had sex with her yet. (Though he clearly assumes the two will progress to that stage and enjoy it.) Is Bay's point that sexism and objectification is a learned response? The product of nurture rather than nature? It's an intriguing element, but the film doesn't expend much effort on exploring this facet.

It might be notable that Jordan is underestimated upon recapture, which allows her to get the drop on her captors. The movie ensures we see even a naïve Jordan as capable of having her own agency and cunning, qualities even her creators and jailers do not anticipate. Do they judge her as Tom does, as just a pretty face? Though considering how innocent and guileless most of the clones are shown to be, it's merely possible that their discounting of her cunning has little to do with gendered biases.

These possibly feminist themes could be reinforced by the film's most chilling moment, perhaps the most disturbing moment in Bay's entire filmography. It is a sequence where a clone gives birth and pleads to hold her baby. Instead, she's given a lethal injection while her physicians show no emotion at all at her passing. There are probably researchers who've bonded more closely with their lab rats than these doctors have with actual human beings. This indifference could certainly have been included as a cautionary tale about how cloning dehumanizes people to the suffering of others. It certainly makes for one of the most affecting moments in Bay's oeuvre.

This moment might also serve as a feminist commentary on how women should be revered for more than just being breeders. In this community, that clone had only one purpose, to be a breeder. By reducing her role to that simple a description, the film forces us to experience the outrage we should feel when women are marginalized into gender-specific and child-rearing roles.

After the severe misstep that was *Bad Boys II*, *The Island* reinforces that Michael Bay is rarely more at home than when he's playing in science-fiction. It offers him a relief from any necessity of keeping all events 100% plausible. It's one of the genres that completely compliments his mythic staging and visual bombast.

It's a sad irony that this imaginative film represents his only notable commercial flop. Domestically, the film took in just under $36 million, his lowest grosser to date. Worldwide it earned just under $163 million, which is a bigger global total than *Bad Boys* ($141 million) and *Pain & Gain* ($82 million). The difference is that those two films only cost $19 million and $26 million to make, respectively. *The Island* had a budget of $126 million, which means after marketing costs and the exhibitors' take are figured in, the movie failed to break even. This would be like seeing Michael Jordan take the basketball court in his prime and manage to shoot only airballs.

The film represents such a staggering commercial disappointment that one really does have to put some stock into Bay's claim that the film wasn't sold very well to the audience. It's also possible that despite the visual flash, the inside-baseball metaphor about the creative process maybe have been too heady for many viewers. It's always sad to see an artist punished for stepping outside his box and trying something more ambitious. In time, perhaps this film will be reevaluated and given its proper due.

Transformers (2007)

Release date: July 3, 2007
Story by John Rogers and Roberto Orci & Alex Kurtzman
Screenplay by Roberto Orci & Alex Kurtzman
Produced by Don Murphy, Tom DeSanto, Lorenzo di Bonaventura, Ian Bryce
Budget: $150 million
Domestic box office: $319.2 million
Global box office: $709.7 million

Michael Bay ruined *Transformers*.

So swears many of my generation. I would have been about four years old when *Transformers* first made its debut as a cartoon series. It ran for several years after that, affording me plenty of time to become familiar with the characters while in kindergarten and first grade. At that age, one's tastes aren't so discerning. The only cartoons I can recall thinking "sucked" were those aimed at (ick!) girls. And even then I was a regular viewer of *She-Ra: Princess of Power* and also owned a She-Ra action figure.

When it came to the "robots in disguise" though, I never owned many of the toys. In fact, I only had a grand total of three Transformers, one of which was a Powermaster Optimus Prime that I didn't get until I was in third grade. My best friend *did* own what felt like the entire line, so I logged more than my fair share of playtime with Optimus Prime, Galvatron, the Dinobots, the Constructicons and so on. I have distinct memories of wanting to go see the 1986 animated movie, but my parents refusing. (This was not out of any objection to cartoon violence. They'd merely had their fill after suffering through two *Care Bears* movies and *He-Man & She-Ra: The Secret of the Sword*. In fact, I *still* get shit from my parents about the *Care Bears* films. Cruddy animation aside, I still get some enjoyment from *The Secret of the Sword* though, so sue me.) The ads didn't exactly make it a secret that Prime was killed, and the post-movie episodes advanced the timeframe forward and introduced a mostly-new cast of robots.

I was six when this went down. Remember what I said about children that age not being able to discern good from bad? Well, I pretty much *hated* the post-movie eps. The colors were darker, the characters were less fun, and even the animation didn't have the same pop. There was a brief ray of hope when Optimus Prime was resurrected in a two-parter, but those ended up being the last new episodes my local station ever carried.

So what I'm getting at is, *Transformers* was already ruined for me in 1986. I'm well aware that subsequent spinoffs like *Beast Wars* kept the characters alive for later generations, but I never paid them much attention. In fact, I'm pretty sure that from about 1989 to 2005, I never even revisited the series in any form.

What changed in 2005? I got Netflix and had some free time on my hands. on a lark, I requested the discs that carried "The Return of Optimus Prime." I don't know if words exist that can convey the vast chasm between my mind's eye recollection of the animation and the actual quality of said production.

In other words, the *Transformers* I loved ruined *Transformers* for me long before any Hollywood director could have. That experience that everyone of my generation is so protective of is a lie built by unrefined tastes, unreliable memory and nostalgia. That's not even getting into the fact that *Transformers* was a cartoon created to sell the toys. Any adult thinking Michael Bay capable of replicating that pre-teen endorphin rush was holding the film to a standard that almost no cinema could meet.

"I thought it was a dumb idea, said Bay when asked what he thought of the project when it was first presented to him.

Compared to the majority of his filmography, *Transformers* is a largely surface-level guilty pleasure. It's executed in a more mainstream style that suggests the helmer was not as bored as he clearly was during *Bad Boys II*. If it wasn't for the unparalled direction Bay shows in handling the complex robot characters, you might mistake this film for the work of his imitators, though. That's not even addressing the fact that the visionary's previous effort had been a fairly pointed jab at the notion of strip-mining old ideas for parts. Perhaps the segment of Bay's audience that comes for the eye candy failed to notice those messages. Hollywood, however, is made up of some of the keenest cinematic minds. The "dog whistles" that Bay included in *The Island* to mock the Hollywood development process almost certainly found their marks. Within the confines of the 310-323-818 area codes, *The Island* was possibly seen to be as pointed an attack on the industry establishment as *Citizen Kane* was on William Randolph Hearst. (I'm not going to explain that one. If you don't get it, do your own research and feel the 12 year-old boy inside you giggle when you learn what "Rosebud" is a very specific poke at.)

I understand some might bristle at comparing director Orson Wells to Michael Bay, one has to cast their minds back and recall that Wells was more than a pitchman for products such as Paul Masson Champagne or Frozen Peas. No, early in his career, *Citizen Kane* was considered quite an accomplishment and his other films were also decently received in that time. Bay certainly has larger hits and a more varied career, but let's not forget the importance of recognizing other artists, no matter how they came to be defined later. (In an interesting connection, Wells appeared in the *Transformers* animated movie as killer planet Unicron.)

Alas, this time Bay's problems were worse than disappointed critics and his audience rejecting his last film. By directing a financial bomb, Bay was at last vulnerable. Coming in succession after his artistic boredom on *Bad Boys II* and creative disappointment on *Pearl Harbor*, *The Island* failing commercially must have been a blow no matter how happy he was with it as a story. Bay had long been known as a guy who always put his audience first, so the commercial performance of his last release could have been a harbinger that he was losing his touch. In a town where you're only good as your last picture, a disappointment like *The Island* can send a director to "movie jail" fast.

Left on his own, Bay might have created a *Transformers* film more reflective of the cartoon, where the robots were clearly front and center with Optimus Prime as the undisputed protagonist and Megatron the obvious antagonist. But for perhaps the first time, Michael Bay was coming onto a project truly vulnerable. For the first time since the original *Bad Boys*, he wasn't the strongest creative voice on a project. He was going to have to do the worst thing for art: compromise.

In examining what works and what doesn't work about *Transformers*, the inescapable conclusion emerges that the largest amount of blame appears to be traceable to one man: Steven Spielberg. A number of sources indicate that it was Spielberg who saw the story as the tale of "a boy and his car." It was a metaphor that co-writer Roberto Orci could understand, telling *The New York Times*, "It's all the things that a car represents in this country. That's a story of stepping into adulthood, stepping into responsibility, possibly a gateway to sex. That is a story — with or without a giant robot."

Particularly in the early stages of his career, Spielberg's films often either focused on children or were aimed at younger audiences. *Raiders of the Lost Ark* was little more than an updated version of the 40s serials that played to the prepubescent crowd. *E.T.* not only focused on children, but completely adopted their perspective. He executive-produced cartoons for children and his "Peter Pan syndrome" was so legendary that there seemed no more apt match of a director and a project than Spielberg taking the helm of *Hook*, the film that dealt with a now-adult Peter Pan returning to Neverland.

Bay was also often accused of arrested development, a frequent criticism of his product being that it was made for teenage boys. This might suggest that their similarly youthful sensibilities would mesh, but there's a key distinction: Spielberg's films reflect a more innocent idealized view of childhood. His teenage (or more accurately, pre-teen) characters don't have their hormones racing. The kids in *The Goonies* haven't discovered sex yet. On at least one superficial level, Bay's movies often speak to teenage boys who have sexual activity as their highest priority.

This is why in Bay's film, the core character is the 16 year-old Sam Witwicky, played by Shia LaBeouf. Sam shares the nucleus of the story with Bumblebee, the disguised Autobot who becomes the first car teenage Sam purchases and later helps him woo sexy classmate Mikaela Banes (played by Megan Fox.)

That immediately changes the focus from what it had been in virtually every previous incarnation. The cartoon shows cast the robots as the stars, with the human characters clearly the sidekicks. By focusing the story through the perspective of a teenage boy, the effect is that we are immediately distanced from the Autobot point of view. Seeing them through human eyes is about as effective as making a *Superman* movie where Jimmy Olsen acts as the audience's eyes and ears. It removes the most exciting thing about the story and makes it a side dish.

This is a mistake Spielberg has repeated throughout his career. *Close Encounters of the Third Kind* could have been a compelling story about alien life making contact with – or perhaps invading – mankind. Instead, the story put the focus on Richard Dreyfuss and his horrible parenting, only delivering the goods at the end of the film. *E.T.* botches its alien story almost as badly, giving zero insight into why the alien race has come to Earth, and failing to explain anything about their race or their agenda. Spielberg makes movies filled with wondrous creatures like aliens, spaceships and sharks – then puts all the focus on the most boring element: people.

And that's what happens here. It triggers a ripple effect throughout the film. An early voiceover from Optimus Prime fills the audience in on the details of a war between the Autobots and Decepticons on the Transformers' planet Cybertron. It devastated the world so badly that the only thing that could restore it was the "All-Spark," a long-lost device capable of great power. In short order, we learn that Decepticons are searching for it on Earth, during a sequence where such an agent attacks a military base in an effort to hack their system and locate the All-Spark.

It's through this sequence that we meet the soldiers who become important characters throughout the story. In a different incarnation of this script, Captain William Lennox (Josh Duhamel) could have been a compelling hero and his team might have been the diverse squad of ragtag heroes that we've seen in *Armageddon*. Unfortunately, the script struggles to find much for them to do for the first half of the film and in the second half, they're largely there to shoot guns. It's not Bay's fault, but it does hurt the film.

The other distracting subplot involves a Pentagon analyst played by Rachael Taylor and how she and a fellow hacker played by Anthony Anderson are detained after attempting to decode the Decepticon signals. It's a side story that doesn't accomplish much that couldn't have been done another way. Bay might deserve some props for depicting a female hacker, but critics were quick to note her looks and style were more appropriate for a supermodel than a Pentagon analyst.

The division of this story and the military story ends up weakening them both. It's a bit like if *The Rock* had kept Stanley Goodspeed stranded on the sidelines as an analyst throughout and then let Sean Connery run around with no one to play off of. Perhaps part of the problem with Bay getting some storytelling elements so right early in his career is that when it comes time to freshen his routine with new approaches, all he's left with are lesser options.

But all we can do is play the cards we're dealt, so let's dive in. I was a script reader for many years and one fairly consistent truth was that a script that opened with a lot of expository voiceover was often one that had storytelling issues from the start. Here it's done to lay some pipe for the Autobot plot, but if we were truly supposed to learn the scope of this universe through Sam, it might have been more appropriate to just reveal it later. Unfortunately, the movie can't start with a giant battle on Cybertron because that would firmly fix the film's protagonists as the robots. Thus, Optimus's narration is merely prologue before we arrive on Earth.

Though the soldiers are really too large a cast to develop in their limited time, Bay does his best to make lemons out of lemonade with the Sam story. He's first shown in school, giving a presentation on his family history. Then he and his father purchase Bumblebee and Sam fumbles around while crashing a party the popular kids are throwing. Mikaela dumps her boyfriend after he ridicules Sam, setting up Sam to offer her a ride home.

Mikaela is actually the most important character in the film (though not the most important character in the *story*. There's a distinction.) It would be easy to take in the visual feast that is Megan Fox, gaze in wonderment at her sun-kissed skin, gape with awe at her toned midriff, stare far too long at her supple—*wait, where was I going with this?!*

Ah, yes. It might have taken until Bay's seventh feature, but we have at last arrived at perhaps the most popular example of a "Michael Bay woman." Such is the power of Megan Fox's performance that viewers convinced themselves that this role personified a long-used stereotype in Bay's work. Even I, as while watching the fourth *Transformers* film, believed that the director's record on female characters had been offensive for quite some time. Not only has this rewatch proved that charge inaccurate with regard to the vast majority of his prior filmography, but visiting this film with an open mind proves that it's barely true here, if at all.

When viewers think of Megan Fox in *Transformers,* they fixate on one scene that became instantly iconic – Mikaela opening up the hood and striking an S-curve pose that hikes up her shirt and draws attention to her exposed stomach. Sam's gaze fixes there and then his eyes become our eyes as we leer upward and then follow back down as she bends over, her rear end now pulling focus. On the most superficial level, we could condemn the film for treating one of its actresses like a piece of meat, but there's more than meets the eye here.

Remember that the camera here becomes less of an objective observer and more reflective of Sam's perspective. It was Spielberg's notion to tell the story through the eyes of a teenage boy, but what Bay has done here has literally translated that to the screen. When a teenage boy looks at a teenage girl as his hormones rage through his body, what he sees is the sexual perfection that Megan Fox is made to embody here. Mikaela is a physical idealization because that perception is the great lie told through the rush of teenage hormones. In fact, there's no reason we should trust that Mikaela actually looks like Megan Fox or is even dressed or posing like her. We have to consider that this is a form of "beer goggles" (or "teenage boy googles") at work here.

It's a technique more easily recognize when you recall Bay's history shooting Victoria's Secret commercials. While men may appreciate the optical delights of seeing beautiful women scantily-clad in lingerie, Bay is not hired to appeal to the male gaze. His job is to sell the lingerie. That means making the image appealing to the client: women. Thus, he's marketing in the fantasy of "Wear these clothes and you will *feel* this sexy." Even there he's trading in an image of non-literal idealization. Bay doesn't shoot from the male gaze for prurient motives, he does it to portray a state of mind. For his commercials it's to entice the women, but here in *Transformers,* it's done to replicate what Sam sees when he looks at his crush. It is the exact opposite of gratuitous exploitation because it completely speaks to character.

Perhaps underlining this is every line of dialogue Mikaela has while checking out Sam's engine. At a glance, she knows what she's doing, giving a rundown of the specs and then boasting that her dad taught her a lot about cars. She could even take it apart, clean it and put it back together again. It's a reveal that subverts any assumption we have that Mikaela is a sex-bomb bimbo. The only people who could possibly miss this message are the ones guilty of leering at Megan Fox.

(In fairness to the pervs, since Bay has demonstrated time and again that he's well aware of how to use particular camera angles and staging to create iconic images, he probably should have realized that the visual would overpower the words here. It's also possible that he did this deliberately as a test to see if the text of the film could overcome the visuals if the dialogue running through the iconic imagery ended up subverting the image.)

Sam "hangs a lantern" on this sexism when he says he wouldn't have pegged [her] for mechanical." She says she doesn't "broadcast it. Guys don't like it when you know more about cars than they do." So we get an explicit demonstration of Sam's close-mindedness, followed up by an all-true real explanation of how women are socialized to not reveal certain interests or skills so that men won't feel threatened.

I began this exploration wondering if Michael Bay has been unfairly maligned all of these years. Now I have to confront the reality that Megan Fox has taken an undue amount of crap for her character for far too long. Time and again, she's not only more likable than Sam, but a fair sight more capable. In a later sequence, Sam is attacked by the Decepticon Frenzy, a smaller, Gremlin-like creation. While the boy struggles haplessly, Mikaela gets a chainsaw and slices the little bugger into pieces. Later during the attack in Mission City, Bumblebee is badly damaged. Though all Sam can think to do is stay with his robot friend, Mikaela actually acts and hotwires a tow truck so that they can load up the Autobot and get him to safety. Later still, she drives so that Bumblebee can shoot, despite not being mobile on his own.

Mikaela is clearly no sidekick or sexy piece of eye candy. She's a strong, capable woman, and yet it is Sam who gets rewarded for his bravery while Mikaela is left as empty-handed as Chewbacca following the presentation of medals after the Death Star assault in *Star Wars*. Heck, say the name "Mikaela Banes" out loud. It's pretty clearly a riff on "Michael Bay." It's so obvious that we should have seen it. Why would the director allow his namesake character to be anything other than the true hero of the film? This should be a theory even more readily accepted by those who think little of Michael Bay because they likely think him to be a raging egomaniac.

If nothing else, you have to say this for Bay - he was handed the marching orders of making the story about the humans, and he managed to use Sam and Mikaela to score more than a few feminist points. Given the Megan Fox-hate that became a pastime on the internet following her rise to fame, one wonders how Bay took to his work being so misinterpreted.

It takes just over an hour before the Autobots other than Bumblebee fully enter the film. It's not quite the midpoint of the two-hour and twenty minute film, but it's close. Even more notably, it's not until about one hour and thirty-seven minutes in that we at last get a view of a frozen Megatron, imprisoned in Hoover Dam. It's a rare film that introduces its true antagonist so late in the story.

But *is* Megatron the true antagonist? The shift to the human characters also allows us to divorce ourselves from the notion that the Autobots are completely pure and noble. At some point we have to wonder, "Why are we letting these two warring alien factions bring their fight into our backyard?" It's not as if the humans have any stake in the All-Spark, yet we are drawn into the Israeli-Palestinian-like conflict between Autobots and Decepticons.

The military story isn't terribly well fleshed out, but in its vestiges, we might see the beginnings of bigger themes. The Autobots and Decepticons are little more than illegal aliens who have smuggled their way onto our planet. The only defense we have against them is the military, which might be read as a call to militarize our borders. The only problem with that is that it doesn't work. The military's weapons are largely useless against the robots.

In fact the only tool that proves truly useful is the coveted power source both factions are fighting over. Given more freedom, I have little doubt that Bay could have sharpened and honed this metaphor so that the overall meaning would be as clear as it is in

Armageddon or *The Island*. Unfortunately, the ending isn't set up all that well. Prime and Megatron battle in Mission City, seemingly with no regard for the human life around them. Sam tries to protect the All-Spark even as Megatron relentlessly hunts him.

Prime explains that he has the ability to destroy the All-Spark if it's placed into his chest, though this act will take Prime's life as well. The mechanics of this are barely justified, so the audience can be forgiven any confusion when Sam somehow shoves it into Megatron's chest. Thus both Megatron and the All-Spark are both destroyed. (His remains and those of the other Decepticons are dumped into the Laurentian Abyss.) It's a tidy ending and as things wind down, we see closure on several fronts, such as Sam and Mikaela becoming a couple and Captain Lennox meeting his baby for the first time. Optimus Prime's closing narration laments that the loss of the All-Spark means that they cannot return life to Cybertron and so they will now have to call Earth home. He sends out a signal to all Autobots, inviting them to join the others there.

Wait, *what?!* So the United States is going to be cool with a whole mess of alien immigrants arriving in the form of killer robots? Prime saw how badly their conflict devastated one city and he makes the call to bring *more* of these machines here?! "We live among [Earth's] people now," Prime says, "Hiding in plain sight, watching over them in secret. Waiting…"

It's an incredibly ominous ending, made even more foreboding by the fact that no one viewing this film through nostalgia-soaked eyes seemed to appreciate the magnitude of what

Prime is responsible for. To be honest, not even most critics seemed to cotton to this. Roger Ebert awarded the film three stars out of four, which was not only decent praise, but fairly unusual in terms of his opinions of Bay's work. *The Rock* had earned three and a half stars from the famous reviewer and *The Island* had garnered three, but it was clear that for Ebert, Bay was an acquired taste. Surprisingly, he found a lot to like in *Transformers*, saying, "It's goofy fun with a lot of stuff that blows up real good, and it has the grace not only to realize how preposterous it is, but to make that into an asset."

Despite some shaky plotting, the film manages to be entertaining. Viewed in context with Bay's filmography, it's hard not to wonder what he'd have accomplished if not hamstrung by Spielberg. Breaking free of Bruckheimer after *Bad Boys II* should have given Bay a chance for rebirth. *The Island* felt like it could have been exactly what *The Rock* was – a strong genre piece that was well-executed, with a few big ideas below the surface. This would seemingly open the door for *Transformers* to have been the second coming of *Armageddon*. Instead, it's more of a *Bad Boys*, with Hollywood's love of franchises threatening to claim one of the most singular voices in big budget action.

Bay's next two films would be *Transformers* movies, and while they are drastically different from each other, there's something sad about seeing a filmmaker confined to a single storytelling universe for so long. As of this writing, four of Bay's 11 feature films are *Transformers* movies, more than a third of his filmography. We have already discussed the brilliance he eventually arrived at in the fourth film, but would we find the middle two chapters to be just dumb entertainment?

Or is there more to them than meets the eye?

Read on.

Transformers: Revenge of the Fallen (2009)

Release date: June 24, 2009
Written by Ehren Kruger & Roberto Orci & Alex Kurtzman
Produced by Don Murphy, Tom DeSanto, Lorenzo di Bonaventura, Ian Bryce
Budget: $200 million
Domestic box office: $402.1 million
Global box office: $836.3 million

Success demands a sequel.

There is no greater truth about the film industry than that one. This makes the result somewhat predictable following *Transformers*'s domestic gross of $319 million and a worldwide total of $709 million. When a studio owns a commodity that has proven value, it is corporate malpractice to fail to keep feeding the hunger of the audience. McDonald's doesn't open for one weekend and then close up shop for good, nor do they change up their menu items significantly. A similar mentality produces the weekly offerings at your neighborhood multiplex. If people paid for something once, they'll probably try it again, so long as you serve it up as indistinguishable from the original as possible.

Also, it needs to be served up quickly, so Paramount targeted a Summer 2009 date for their second *Transformers* film, allowing about two years between films. Two years sounds like a lot until you realize that the complex visual effects necessitate nearly a year of post-production work. Also complicating matters in the latter half of 2007 was a looming strike of the Writers Guild of America. Their contract was set to expire on November 1 and if a strike occurred, as many expected it would, nothing could be written for the film until a new contract was negotiated. This was a threat that every summer tentpole set for 2009 release was facing.

The original writers from the first film, Roberto Orci and Alex Kurtzman, originally turned down offers to return before eventually signing a deal that enlisted both them and *The Ring* screenwriter Ehren Kruger to work together on the film. *The Los Angeles Times* claimed this deal was worth $8 million.

In an interview with the website *First Showing*, Orci recalled the race against the clock they faced as the strike approached. "It was insane. We literally started breaking stories two weeks before the strike. In two weeks, we generated an outline. It was pens down the minute the strike hit. We didn't deal with Michael at all during the strike." The movie was prepped off of the outline and Orci further related that they were prohibited from writing until the strike ended – which turned out to be a mere two months before shooting began. This meant that there was no time to do anything but execute that hastily-devised original plan.

Because of this, *Transformers: Revenge of the Fallen* is a less complete work of art that the vast majority of Bay's filmography. A complex film like *Armageddon* was a true masterpiece because Bay had the time he needed to hone the script – with many writers – and refine his themes over time. Though Bay has sometimes complained after the fact that he didn't get to complete post-production to his liking, his films still hold up because of the solid foundation present in most of his scripts.

Thus, this would make *Revenge of the Fallen* an incredibly tempting target for scorn if it also did not give us a peek at what a Bay film looks like without its final touch-ups. This is akin to getting to x-ray the Mona Lisa and examine the pencil sketch below the painting.

Critics certainly didn't appreciate this at the time. The film received a rating of just 19% on Rotten Tomatoes, with Roger Ebert calling it "a horrible experience of unbearable length." Other reviewers were equally abusive. *The Village Voice's* Robert Wilonsky claimed the film was a "bewildering, noisy, sloppy, cynical piece of work, a movie that sneers at the audience for 147 minutes and expects us to lap it up as entertainment—and be grateful. This is blockbuster porn absent even the suggestion of care or concern for anything that might resemble "a point," save the obvious one to move more Hasbro action figures and animated-series DVD boxed sets. In a word: distasteful."

Rolling Stone's review was not atypical of the rest of the response. "Go ahead, have your senses senselessly pounded for two and a half hours…. I know there are still 17 months to go, but I'm thinking *Transformers 2* has a shot at the title Worst Movie of the Decade."

Given the crunch with which the film was conceived, one has to wonder if some of this wasn't part of the point Bay was trying to achieve. There was no single greater influence on this film than the

Writers Guild strike, and having lived in Los Angeles during that strike, I can tell you that public sentiment was very much on the writers' side. We've talked before about how much Michael Bay respects the craft of writing. He's such a fan of writers that he employed a small army of them on *Armageddon* alone. Is it really far-fetched to presume that the complete narrative failure of *Revenge of the Fallen* is actually a deliberate commentary on how foolish it is to discount the contribution of writers?

At the time, Bay could not have predicted that this film would eventually prove to be an even larger hit than the first, at least in a commercial sense. In a critical sense, if Bay was out to make a film that every reviewer would line up to piss on, he succeeded. The numerous reviews that ripped apart the story show that on a basic level, these tastemakers reacted in the way the director wanted. They just failed to make the leap that there was a point to the incoherence, even if some websites pointed out how the strike impacted an already hurried script.

It also helps to remember that the success of the first film stood in such sharp contrast to Bay's *The Island* that its inexplicable success must have been another stab into Bay's heart. It wasn't as if he made many drastic alterations to his style, nor was *Transformers* full of established stars. In the face of those facts, it would be harder to ignore the likelihood that it was the toy brand itself that beckoned the audience to show up.

Like it or not, human failings will creep into an artist's work. Along with a number of other half-developed themes, *Revenge of the*

Fallen strongly betrays Michael Bay's own sense of self-loathing. With two years in between the films, audiences could be forgiven for missing the most overt clues buried in the film. Watching the sequel in close succession with the original brings it all home, though.

Mikaela Barnes was one of the strongest characters in the original film. Though her portrayer's fetching appearance obscured that, the onus for that failing is on the beholder, not the beheld. We discussed Bay's identification with this namesake character at some length in the last section, making a full recap unnecessary here. It is probably worth reminding that the one occasion where the camera egregiously leered at Megan Fox, it was clearly presented as representing Sam's teenage boy point-of-view.

Mikaela is introduced in the sequel via an even more exploitative shot, mounting a motorcycle in such a way that the camera moving in from behind has little choice but to give her up-thrust derriere prominence in the scene. It's pure eye candy on a level that Mikaela somewhat, making us regard her only for her superficial charms.

Much in the way Bay has often only been appreciated on a surface level.

The first film presented a three-dimensional woman who surprised the teenage boy (a stand-in for Bay's biggest audience) when she actually understood what was going on "under the hood." Mikaela's treatment in *Revenge of the Fallen* at last shows that years of critiques have finally gotten to Bay. He's essentially throwing his hands in the air and saying, "Fine! You look at me and only see pretty pictures and explosions? Well that's what you're going to get!" Through Mikaela, Bay is working out his issues not with women, but with the imaginary Michael Bay whom the press delights in sparring with. It's a bit like watching Clark Kent grapple with Superman in *Superman III*. Whatever Mikaela represented to Bay during the first film was transformed and corrupted by the reaction to that film. In response, Bay reconceives her to represent the albatross of "being Michael Bay." It's perhaps not his most mature effort, but it is a revealing one.

This time around, Mikaela is a lot less essential to the plot. Her most significant contribution is capturing the Decepticon Wheelie, but beyond that, she's mostly along for the ride. Her relationship with Sam is given a few uninteresting roadblocks, chiefly that Sam finds it difficult to say "I love you" to his goddess of a girlfriend even after two years together. With more time to hone the script, this could have evolved to show Sam saying that in a way that expresses just how much there is "more" to Mikaela "than meets the eye." As executed, it ends up being little more than a way to manufacture emotional resonance in the climax when they admit their feelings to each other.

Sam's own arc plays like a rough draft too. He's going off to college in this film and there's some angst when Optimus Prime reaches out to Sam for help when the young man is just trying to live a normal life. The script goes through some contortions to put Sam at the center of events when he comes into contact with a piece of the All-Spark, filling his head with all manner of Cybertronian knowledge and symbols. The Decepticons soon retrieve a piece of the All-Spark to revive Megatron and then pursue Sam for the knowledge in his head. (Some possible subtext about the male lead being valued for his mind rather than his body goes unexamined.) They capture Sam long enough to pull symbols from his head that will lead them to the source of Energon, which the Transformers use to power themselves.

In the backstory, we learn that a group of seven Primes traveled across the universe to activate Sun Harvesters and create Energon. Since this destroyed those suns, they swore not to do this for inhabited planets. One of them broke with the others and set up a Harvester on Earth long ago. The other six defeated him – renaming him The Fallen - before he could activate it and imprisoned him before sacrificing themselves to hide "The Matrix of Leadership," which is capable of turning on the Harvester.

To put it mildly, there are a lot of unfilled holes in this backstory, starting with the lack of explanation for why The Fallen found it absolutely necessary to set up shop on Earth. If any star will do, why would he be so determined to destroy our sun when he could just move on to the next solar system? The necessity of the other six Primes sacrificing themselves to protect the Matrix is also unclear. Since we're later told that "only a Prime" can kill The Fallen, if the other Primes take themselves off the game board, doesn't that make The Fallen a bigger threat by default? No matter how dangerous he is, there are six of them ready to take him on.

Surely a better solution than mass suicide would be to just kill the rogue?

It's also murky what distinguishes a "Prime" from other Transformers. As part of Optimus's name, it seemed to indicate a higher status. This was appropriate given his position as the leader, but the fact that The Fallen fears Primes indicates there's something inherently different about a Prime. The script never gets around to explaining what that is, though, and Prime needs an unrelated power-up in order to be ready to take on The Fallen in the end. When I was a reader, I'd call a script with these sort of weak foundations a "because I said so" script. In those, things only happen because the writer declares it so, with no logical support from within the screenplay itself.

It's not unusual to see that sort of half-formed logic in early drafts, but they are glaring, completely unobscured lapses when put in a feature film. Given the circumstances in which the film was rushed into production, one could forgive the first-draft nature of the shooting script, but so much of the material involving The Fallen was completed in post with the VFX, along with voiceover work that had to have been done long after shooting was completed. It's hard to believe that a little ADR couldn't have smoothed over some of this backstory.

That means that the most likely explanation for these gaping plot holes is that Michael Bay wanted them to be there. With the film a known casualty of the Writers' Strike, all of this was a charade to underline just how valuable writers are to the process. One doesn't produce such huge story holes unless they are clearly deliberate performance art. Michael Bay might not have been able to stop production in solidarity with the striking writers, but he certainly could use his influence to cripple the film as a show of support.

Still not convinced? Perhaps you cling to the belief that these backstory gaffes were easily overlooked? That's just the beginning.

The reason the Decepticons need the Energon is so that they can give life to Decepticon "hatchlings." These creatures are glimpsed once in the film, when Megatron meets with The Fallen and Starscream in an African hideout. They resemble embryonic beings in small sacs, which gives an oddly organic sort of feeling to creatures that are entirely mechanical. It's a birthing process that has more in common with the beings in *Alien* or *Gremlins* than machines you'd assume would be constructed in some sort of factory. In terms of the film, it's a total non-sequitir, made more egregious by the fact that since this entire sequence was a VFX job, valuable time was spent creating these beings for no real purpose.

The character of Alice is an equally nonsensical addition to the cast. First introduced as a hot college classmate of Sam's, she's soon revealed to be a Decepticon in human disguise. This is the first and only time we see such a character in the four films, and it feels like giving the Decepticons the ability to blend in among normal people has huge implications that are never dealt with. Most of the Decepticons throughout the series are either very large robots or very small machines like Wheelie. Alice doesn't fit either category and more notably, she's the only Transformer who seems capable of mimicking human flesh. We might be able to assume that she was a creation of the Decepticons hiding on Earth, but for the fact that the hatchling scene makes it clear they can't create new robots without an Energon source. Thus Alice's origins remain a mystery and she's defeated rather easily for a Decepticon. This again feels like a stray notion never fully integrated into the script.

(I would wade into the *Transformers* wiki to see if any non-canon explanations of her backstory exist, but the last time I went there it took two search-and-rescue teams to extract me from the quicksand that is *Transformers* extended universe continuity)

The sheer preponderance of inexplicable elements makes it less likely that they were included by chance. No matter the time crush, no matter the pressures, no film is this sloppy by accident. This is a movie where Sam dies and goes to some kind of robot heaven where the spirits of the Primes tell him that he's always been destined to earn the Matrix of Leadership. He's resurrected and in doing so, the Matrix is reconstituted in a way that allows him to use it to revive a temporarily dead Optimus Prime.

It's also yet another film where Megatron - who in the cartoon was the Lex Luthor to Prime's Superman - gets back-grounded. In this case, he's overshadowed by The Fallen as the real threat to such a degree that it wouldn't be hard to remove him from the story altogether. What made it to screen was a story full entirely of "wouldn't it be cool" moments, without the careful plotting and character depth to navigate the film from A to B. Bay is a brilliant idea guy, but you can't build a house with only bricks. Mortar is also essential. Did we learn nothing from the story of the Three Pigs?

For the most part, Bay turns into the skid, making sure the audience remains aware of this. He doesn't try his *Bad Boys II* trick of amping up the style in every scene just to keep himself interested. He's fully capable of that and his restraint here shows that he wanted this film to look as much like the previous film so that he could drive home the contrast in the story construction. The awful critical reception had to be what he wanted, to provoke the audience into demanding more from their summer tentpoles than glorious explosions

The few hints of greater depth can be found in The Fallen's backstory. His very name recalls the term "fallen angel," a phrase often used to refer to Satan. The symbolism isn't deepened much beyond that, though this connection was presumably another detail that would have been sharpened in later rewrites. This Biblical connection likely would have been developed alongside Prime's death and Christ-like resurrection. This is one of the truly frustrating things about this film – you can see the bigger ideas jotted down, but in sort of a "drunken ramblings scribbled on a cocktail napkin" sort of way.

Bay's dissatisfaction with simplistic summer blockbusters is written all over this film. It's evident that any parts of the film that weren't conceived out of disgust for mindless blockbusters were probably provoked by self-loathing for being the orchestrator of such a Frankenstein monster. Perhaps at this point in his life, he felt that a kamikaze attack was the only way to cripple the tentpole mentality once and for all. A high profile dud of this caliber would surely promote change, possibly even herald the return of a different kind of filmmaking.

Following its June 2009 opening, *Transformers: Revenge of the Fallen* earned $402 million domestically on a $200 million budget. Worldwide, it took in $836 million, which was $127 million more than its predecessor. Bay had tried to strike the franchise down, but it only became more powerful.

Transformers: Dark of the Moon (2011)

Release date: June 29, 2011
Written by Ehren Kruger
Produced by Don Murphy, Tom DeSanto, Lorenzo di Bonaventura, Ian Bryce
Budget: $195 million
Domestic box office: $352.4 million
Global box office: $1.12 billion

As part of my college film education, I was once required to view a film called *Sullivan's Travels*. This 1942 Preston Sturges picture was about a director named John Sullivan who has become restless after making a series of silly but successful comedies. His passion project is a heavy drama about the less-fortunate, based on a novel called *O Brother, Where Art Thou?* (Yes, this is where Joel and Ethan Coen took the name of their 2000 film.) To further the authenticity of this project, he decides to live for a time as a homeless tramp.

Complications ensue when another tramp steals the shoes in which Sullivan has hidden his ID and Sullivan himself develops amnesia. A scuffle results in his being sentenced to a labor camp and as he regains his memory, he gets a lesson in how the "simple" sort of comedies he used to make actually bring great joy to people. He and the other prisoners are shown a screening of a Disney cartoon comedy and he's amazed when the movie prompts uproarious laughter. In fact, it's enough laughter to briefly raise their spirits. He gets an epiphany that the work he'd dismissed as foolish can touch an audience just as profoundly as the most serious drama.

When he was hired to work on the first *Transformers*, Michael Bay made it clear he'd never been a fan of the cartoon or the franchise. Fealty to earlier versions is not a prerequisite for a feature director, nor should it be. Still, that doesn't change the fact he was coming into the franchise as an outsider and clearly struggled to find his way inside the material more than he had with previous films. The sequel was plagued with its own problems, and as we discussed, Bay's own self-loathing comes through. All of this makes it more remarkable that the third film, *Transformers: Dark of the Moon*, ends up being the most strongly-constructed film in the franchise yet.

I bring up *Sullivan's Travels* because it seems probable that after resenting the popularity of his less intellectual films, Bay realized that the escapism his movies provide are equally appreciated. To some extent, Bay had always used this superficial flash-and-bang to appeal to his audience on the most base level. This time, the over-performance of a film that might as well have been a two-and-a-half-hour demo reel for Industrial Light and Magic perhaps showed him that audiences will always hunger for empty calories. It's my personal theory that he felt he owed them at least one straight-up adventure and set to work at playing within the toybox his viewers so deeply coveted.

The balance between the human characters and the machines is well-maintained, but more importantly, the script's story is more unified. Where the first film branched off into three disparate tracks that eventually converged, the third film makes the story of recovered Autobot leader Sentinel Prime the clear A-story and then ensures that the B-story featuring Sam collides with it relatively early in the film.

The film is also helped by tying Sam's participation to character-based reasons over MacGuffin-based ones. He's the only human who Optimus Prime truly trusts, which leads the villains to attempt to exploit him in order to undermine Prime. He's not special because of something he got by happenstance, whether that's a car or a brain download of alien knowledge. This time around, Sam is useful because of the relationships he's forged and what he has done. In the earlier films, any idiot could have bought Bumblebee or gotten the mind-zap from the All-Spark fragment. There is only one human whom Optimus Prime trusts, though, and that relationship is built on two years of history. He also ends up being one of the few people to notice a connection between a lot of murdered scientists and the Decepticon plan. With Sam old enough to have a little more agency, Bay finally is able to use him the way he's used his heroic leads in other films.

Certainly one element of the film that must be discussed is the removal of Mikaela Banes from the storyline. After her treatment in the second film, Michael Bay's stand-in is missing entirely from this go-round. Interestingly, the film not only specifies that Sam and Mikaela broke up but that she dumped him. A bitter Sam remarks that with his current girlfriend Carly, he's "finally found someone who appreciates me for me." Could it be that the banishment of the old avatar of Michael Bay represents the director coming into this film with a different attitude than the two previous adventures? That the "old" Bay is replaced with someone who accepts the franchise for what it is? It's also likely no accident that while Mikaela was entirely an invention of the first Bay *Transformers* film, Carly is actually a character in *Transformers* canon who goes all the way back to the original cartoon show. This perhaps symbolizes Bay's acceptance and appreciation of the wider mythology. Or it shows that Bay and writer Ehren Kruger can use Wikipedia just as well as I can.

At one point I had theorized that by replacing actress Megan Fox with Victoria's Secret supermodel Rosie Huntington-Whiteley was Bay's effort at a sly joke about how it doesn't matter at all who plays the part. The actors are seemingly so interchangeable that there must be a message in the fact that one of the series' most beloved characters could be replaced by a lingerie model with no serious effect on the story. While it's true a number of reviewers also made snide remarks to this effect, after studying the totality of Bay's filmography and the previous two *Transformers* films in particular, I'm less of a believer in this pet theory.

Dark of the Moon was released in 2011, not coincidentally the year of the final space shuttle missions. *Armageddon* already had shown us that Bay possessed deep respect and admiration for the space program, so much that that earlier film may as well have functioned as a recruiting ad for NASA. Space exploration was in the process of being mothballed as this film came together, and one doesn't have to look too hard to find a cynical tone towards America's space program. The film posits that the race to the moon in the sixties came about only because NASA detected the crash of an Autobot ship on the moon in 1961. It was their determination to get to it before the Russians that provoked the moon landing so that they'd have first shot at exploring the wreckage.

In real life, the moon landing was one of man's greatest achievements, a symbol of determination to fulfill a goal set by President Kennedy in 1961 to land "a man on the moon, and returning him safely to the Earth." It was similar to the old joke about why one climbs a mountain – because it's there. In the *Transformers* history, this was less about the accomplishment for its own sake and motivated more by politics and power. We would not have gone to the moon if there was not something there we thought we could plunder. A few other tributes to NASA appear in the film, most notably a cameo from Edwin "Buzz" Aldrin, the second man to walk on the moon. Through these nods to America's pioneering spirits, we can begin to understand at least some of Bay's motivations for coming back for a third movie.

The plot concerns the discovery of a dormant Autobot in the ship crashed on the moon. Optimus Prime identifies him as Sentinel Prime, the former leader of the Autobots who was lost during the war on Cybertron. His ship contained a device that could have ended the war – the means to make a "Space Bridge" joining two points in space to transport large objects across great distances. Optimus is able to revive Sentinel Prime using the Matrix of Leadership and shortly thereafter, Sentinel betrays him. Ages ago, he had cut a deal with Megatron in order to ensure the survival of their race. Now Sentinel and Megatron take over Chicago and begin setting pillars that will open the space bridge and bring Cybertron to Earth. In addition to Earth's resources being plundered to rebuild Cybertron, the human population will be made into slave labor.

Sam helps figure all of this out and also discovers that Carly's boss Dylan Gould is a human collaborator with the Decepticons. Since Gould is holding Carly captive, Sam resolves to get into the heavily-fortified Chicago and rescue her. He gets backup in the form of a team led by Col. Lennox and retired Master Sgt. Epps.

Putting aside the fact that there are a lot of characters introduced and reintroduced along the way, the story is pretty straight-forward. Perhaps some early material focusing on Sam's parents and his struggles to get a job could have been trimmed, but those moments are also essential to humanizing Sam. It's challenging to build sympathy for a kid who owns a robot car and has had two mega-beautiful girlfriends in his short life. Bay needs to make this guy an underdog again so that the younger audience can identify with him instead of waiting to give him a reason for his ubiquitous "No-no-no-no-no-no-no!" chant.

At one point he interviews for a job working for a businessman played by John Malkovich. Sam has been through so many job interviews that he loses it a little bit when he realizes the position is little more than working in the mail room. Like any entitled twenty-something, he flaunts accomplishments that mean little to his interviewer. (In this case, he touts the fact that President Obama gave him a medal. I ask you, does Malkovich's aging capitalist look like a guy who'd be impressed by anything associated with President Obama? Sam kind of deserves to lose the job just for his inability to read the room there.) Malkovich appraises the young man and says that his problem is that he doesn't want "this job. You want the job after this job." The problem is that the mailroom job is standing in-between him and that job. This dialogue might take on more resonance after one realizes that by the time he made this, Bay had been itching to direct a movie called *Pain & Gain* for a while, only to have the second and third *Transformers* films take priority. The scene is a nod the necessary evil that Bay had to accept in order to make his passion project. I too am hoping to make a low-budget, character-driven film, and as such, am dreading the day a studio calls me up and demands I helm a billion-dollar franchise film as a prerequisite to my art.

      There also is the other subtext that even as Sam's adventures with the Transformers has brought him accolades like a Presidential Medal, his life has been largely ruined by those same adventures. He's died once, his parents and girlfriend have been imperiled frequently and he's the number one target the Decepticons go after when trying to get at the Autobots. Sam is basically the damsel in distress for these movies. I guarantee that if the films has space to include the Decepticon Astrotrain, at one point Sam would have been tied to train tracks that heralded the villain's entry. No matter how you look at it, mayhem follows wherever Sam goes, which makes befriending him an even riskier prospect than attending a dinner party with Jessica Fletcher.

For the second straight film, Megatron is overshadowed by a larger threat, with Sentinel Prime filling almost the exact same role that The Fallen occupied in the last film. Sentinel Prime is another traitorous Prime, though his sin is motivated less by individual conquest and more by the greater good. He's only trying to save his race, which means that from a certain point of view, Optimus is the enemy because his loyalty isn't to his own people.

One consistent message from this film is that Optimus is a bad leader. He's easily duped into recovering and reviving Sentinel Prime, his admiration for his former mentor blinding him to the possibility that Sentinel is no longer allied with him. The government places their trust in Prime and he fails them worse than whoever was responsible for designing the Obamacare website. He has a shining moment when he successful fools everyone into believing he and the Autobots are leaving Earth. This gives the Decepticons a chance to seemingly kill the Autobots by destroying their ship right after launch. The Autobots show up in the third act to help liberate Chicago, but there's a long stretch of the battle where Optimus Prime just plain disappears. It's like the VFX budget needed to take a fifteen-minute smoke-break. Before some of you nitpick that joke by citing all the Chicago-based destruction during that interval, I'd posit that Bay's commitment to realism likely mandated he actually put the Windy City under siege and only added the Autobots and Decepticons into action. Those are real explosions, people!

The moments without the Optimus Prime are less noticeable since the human characters are given more interesting set-pieces in this city battle than they received in the first film. Sam gets to Carly and then he and the soldiers have to evade the Decepticon Shockwave while in a building that's half-tipped over. Bay has a lot of fun staging this battle, having the characters slide across the sloped floor, trying to stop before they slide out shattered windows on the other side. I guarantee you that somewhere there is probably footage of Bay personally testing out the action of sliding down this sloped floor, probably while letting out a boyish "Wheeeeeeee!" as he does so.

Bay works a little more suspense into his action sequences this time, utilizing longer takes for moments like when the characters take cover to evade a renegade robot's eyeline. This is likely a concession to the 3D effects, which are far less effective when applied to Bay's usual rapid cutting style. He's forced to hold onto shots longer, which alters the general pacing of the set-pieces. Thus, the action gains dimension in more ways than just those afforded through the 3D glasses.

Ever since *The Rock*, it's been worth examining Bay's films to see if how his commentary on the military and government has evolved. By this film, government lackey Simmons, the human villain in the first film played by John Turturro, has graduated to full-blown ally. He is shown to be far more prosperous since his disgrace and drumming out of the public sector. In the second film, he was merely a conspiracy theorist working in a deli. Now he's written a successful tell-all conspiracy book about the Transformers and appears to be swimming in cash. After Sam reaches out to him, he ends up assisting the Director of National Intelligence, played by Frances McDormand.

Simmons, is often portrayed as the level-headed one who appears to have a better handle on the situation than the other bureaucrats. It's a role that could have only been convincingly filled by literally anyone not drawing a federal paycheck. He's less of a comic relief this time around, or at least, the script doesn't encourage us to laugh *at* him quite so much. It's a possible criticism of those who devote their lives to being public servants, or at least a message that the individual is best served by such tenure being limited and that their real value might be found in the private sector. This would mesh with *The Rock's* theme of how the good soldiers got screwed by their country. Perhaps not insignificantly, the first person to really help Sam get into Chicago to save Carly is retired Air Force Chief Epps. It's not an aggressively-developed theme, but it is somewhat notable.

Another notable bit of duality is how the film contrasts characters who act in their own best interests rather than that of their race. Patrick Dempsey's slimy Dylan Gould betrays all of humanity with his deal with the Decepticons, fulfilling a pact his father made years earlier. This moved me, honestly. I hope to one day have children who will honor me enough to enslave a whole planet in the name of a deal I made, mostly like while I was drunk or trying to impress a woman. (Also, did this deal require a paper contract? Do you think they had a notary? Maybe the notary stamping device was a Decepticon? Does anyone else really want to see this scene too?)

Anyway, Gould kidnaps Carly as a way of motivating Sam to act in their interests and it's later spelled out that he sold out mankind so that he could avoid becoming slave labor once Cybertron is brought into the solar system. (He apparently missed the memo that the Decepticons tend to kill all their human minions once they've outlived their usefulness.) Even before Gould is exposed as evil, he's played as a slick bastard, but when seen in all his slimy opportunist glory he becomes the most unlikable villain in three films. He's akin to the Jewish Ghetto Police during the Holocaust, who helped the Nazis round up other Jews and ferry them to the concentration camps. If there's one group history never looks kindly upon, it's collaborators.

Sentinel Prime also betrays his "race" in a sense, switching sides from the Autobots to the Decepticons. In that case, though, he's acting less from selfish means and more out of consideration for the Transformer race as a whole. He's given more nobility than Gould, to the point where even in his final moments he feels he was justified. Defeated and at Optimus Prime's mercy, he pleads, "Optimus... all I ever wanted... was the survival of our race... You must see why I had to betray you." Optimus is unmoved, raising his gun and saying, "You didn't betray me, Sentinel. You betrayed yourself," before coldly executing Sentinel.

I'll repeat that – the hero of this story straight-up executes a subdued villain. This is not a "heat-of-battle" killing, nor is it a kill-or-be-killed situation. Optimus Prime commits an incredibly brutal act that would be even more shocking if it played out with two human characters. This comes after he delivers an even more visceral end to Megatron, decapitating him and ripping out the equivalent of his spine. The Megatron execution might be even the more unnerving of the two, as the villain is literally begging for mercy as Optimus goes in for the kill. True, Megatron has been a thorn in the Autobots' side for three straight films, but the filmmakers made a conscious choice not to make the killing more justified via the circumstances here.

When the Superman reboot *Man of Steel* came out in 2013, many fans of the character took exception to a key moment of the climax when Superman killed General Zod by snapping his neck. This followed a brutal battle that laid waste to much of Metropolis and climaxed in Grand Central Station. There, Superman desperately tried to keep Zod from frying a family with his heat vision, eventually having to kill Zod to prevent that. Critics of the movie decried the filmmakers need to make Superman darker and edgier, arguing that he never killed before (ignoring the fact that at least three of the Reeve films feature Superman taking a life in some way.) However, that situation really did feel like a kill-or-be-killed. From everything that built up to it, Superman had no choice because there was no prison that could hold Zod, nor did Zod give any indications he would even entertain surrendering. Even with these justifications, one can still understand some fans at least raising a concern about Superman's actions.

To the best of my memory and research, there was no such outcry at Optimus Prime's act of cold-blooded double-murder. Perhaps the violence is muted by the fact that perpetrator and victims are all machines. They're already de-humanized in the audience's minds, which allows moments like Sentinel Prime ripping off Optimus's entire arm to go by without much reaction. There may not be blood, but it's still a violent act. Multiple robot executions and dismemberments are littered throughout the film, making the film violent to such a degree that if the same fights were staged with human combatants, the film would have earned a hard-R from the MPAA ratings board.

This may be another instance where Bay might be making a very deliberate sly remark regarding violence in film. We have already established much of the problem is Optimus's doing, though inadvertently. Even though he's part of the ultimate solution, the humans contribute a great deal to taking down the Space Bridge. It's easy enough to believe they might well have stepped up on their own if Optimus had not been there. Since the audience is already primed to look at Optimus with a jaundiced eye, his dishonorable actions at the end of the film might be there to reinforce that he's not a hero in the truest sense of the word. The film doesn't overtly highlight this notion, but by the time of the next sequel it will be unavoidable.

If that is an intended takeaway, then the even broader critical commentary is plausibly that the summer blockbuster as a whole leads the audience to revere the wrong kind of hero. This would be a direct consequence of the dehumanizing of the characters and of human life in general. The robot brutality is a metaphor for this depersonalization – the audience doesn't bat an eye at Megatron's spine being ripped out because he's not "real" – but how many characters in a tentpole film does an audience generally apply that degree of empathy to? The difference is that the censors likely apply different standards, but in terms of the audience reaction, the disconnect may be less profound.

The fact that Optimus Prime's actions failed to make the waves that the Zod neck-snap did shows that audiences are already on the road to being desensitized to certain types of violence. This may have informed the direction that Bay took the Autobots in with the next film *Age of Extinction*. That film truly only works if you accept that the Autobots are actually the real villains of the entire franchise.

Despite that, the film is an entertaining adventure story and holds up better than any of its predecessors in the franchise. This isn't peak-Bay, but he at least broadens his style and proves he can still put together a slick crowd-pleaser that doesn't feel like an assault on the senses. I find the more intellectual works of *Armageddon* and *The Island* to be the more compelling films, but as an energetic romp, *Transformers: Dark of the Moon* hits more than it misses.

Pain & Gain (2013)

Release date: April 26, 2013
Based on <u>Pain & Gain: This is a True Story</u> by Pete Collins
Screenplay by Christopher Markus & Stephen McFeely
Produced by Michael Bay, Ian Bryce, Donald De Line
Budget: $26 million
Domestic box office: $49.9 million
Global box office: $86 million

After three straight *Transformers* movies, probably no one was more tired of that franchise than Michael Bay. On the other hand, with three enormous hits on top of each other, he indisputably had what is generally known around Hollywood as "fuck you" money. This is usually the part of the arc where the successful Hollywood player enacts the time-honored tradition of blowing all that power and goodwill on a vanity project that's completely divorced from the qualities that made an audience fall in love with them. This is how someone like John Travolta manages to earn a lot of cred in *Pulp Fiction*, then turns around and spends all of it making *Battlefield Earth*.

But then Bay has always been savvier than most of his peers and his skill at knowing what an audience wants ensures that he'll continue to be employable. He could have directed a $150 million version of *My Dinner With Andre* that closed two weeks into its run and he'd still find an open director's chair for the next *Transformers* installment. As much as the killer robot franchise provided him with golden handcuffs, they also made a convenient parachute. If anything, he was better positioned to absorb the impact of a failure now even when compared to his previous simultaneous and artistic peak of *Armageddon*.

So if you're going to take a risk, why not make it a big one?

As interviews from the time of the release of the first *Transformers* film document, Bay had considered a change-up as far back as the completion of that project. When *Entertainment Weekly* asked about his future plans, he replied, "A couple things are on the horizon, but [maybe] I'll do my little movie that I can knock out, because we all think we're going to have a strike." Pressed for further details, he expounded, "*Pain and Gain*. It's a true story, happened in Florida. Just love the characters. It's these guys who work at a gym, and nothing's good enough. They're all looking for the American Dream, and they end up kidnapping. It's like a mixture of *Fargo* and *Pulp Fiction*, but it's all true. And they're knuckleheads. The whole point is no one's happy with what they've got. It's a fun character piece. No action. One car crash."

As it happened, the next two *Transformers* films took priority. Both of them were so successful that the studio was eager to have him behind the wheel of a fourth installment, so Bay used that leverage. He agreed to make a fourth *Transformers* film if Paramount would fund his relatively low-budget passion project. As Bay's description above suggests, the material seems more suited to the Coen brothers or Quentin Tarantino than the showman whose work is often referred to as "Bay-hem." The script drew inspiration from the real-life kidnappings and murders committed by a gang of

Miami body builders in the mid-1990s, as documented in a series of newspaper articles. The gang was led by Daniel Lugo and Noel Doorbal (played in the film by Mark Wahlberg and Anthony Mackie, respectively), who kicked off their crime spree by kidnapping businessman Marc Schiller and holding him prisoner for a month. During that time he was subjected to torture while they tried to extort him.

Once they stole his house and his offshore banking account, the gang made several attempts to kill him. First they forced him to down sleeping pills and alcohol and put him behind the wheel of his car after setting it on fire. Even after ramming a utility pole, he survived and staggered from the wreck. The gang then ran over him twice and left him for dead.

That was their failing as Schiller woke up in a hospital only to find that the police didn't buy his story at all and had no interest in pursuing the suspects. This lead him to hire a private investigator named Ed Du Bois, but by the time Du Bois built a case against the bodybuilders, they had already kidnapped and killed two more people: Frank Griga and Krisztina Furton

The kind of violence Bay is known for generally isn't the dark and brutal variety. To date, his most grounded films had been the *Bad Boys* pictures and even they generally adhered to the rules of a well-worn buddy-cop genre. This would be a story where escapism didn't come built into the premise. Even when Bay branched into more complex and intelligent themes, such as in *Armageddon* and *The Island*, there was still the veneer of the pure blockbuster. This offered no such camouflage, a fact which Bay embraced like a duck to water. In a February 2012 post on his website, he announced the film by playing up how it would be much simpler, calling it "a great character piece." A month later he would expound, "It is being made for $22 million. I want to do this one cheap. Not get muddled in the stuff. It's about the characters on this one. I'm taking director scale pay as well."

This shouldn't be misunderstood as Bay feeling that his earlier films were lesser works in any way though. After the first *Transformers*, he recounted to *Entertainment Weekly* a conversation he had with a member of the Hollywood Foreign Press. "she [asks me], 'Wouldn't you want to do more of an art movie, like something that's hard to do?' And I said, 'Are you kidding me? …It is so much harder to do, these type of [big action] movies, than a little art movie in the south of France. I mean, if you can take something that doesn't exist and make it look like it's got a soul, that's art."

Bay was driving his film career into the territory where most blockbuster filmmakers begin, effectively reversing the presumed trajectory. In doing so, he restored an element that most artists must be confronted with in order to thrive: limitations. While at this point it's something of a cliché to attack M. Night Shyamalan's later films, it's hard to deny that his work became less interesting the fewer people he had to answer to. Michael Bamberger's fascinating book focusing on the making of *The Lady in the Water*, called *The Man Who Heard Voices*, is a compelling look at how Shyamalan stopped accepting outside advice and input when it contradicted his desire, even if that advice was well-meaning. It's a fascinating portrait of how an artist travels down the road to self-indulgence.

I don't necessarily believe that all self-indulgence is a bad thing. However, when a creator is no longer beholden to any other authority, their creative process can become complacent. Their first instincts now go unchallenged, so perhaps raw ideas are never polished and shaped into the gems they might have become through the normal creative process. With no need to fight for or justify certain artistic decisions, complacency replaces innovation and passion. And coming off of his third *Transformers* film, Bay probably could feel his instincts dulling.

Now that we've explored why Bay would take on a smaller project at all, the question becomes, why this project specifically? This script exhibits a commitment to character development unlike any other Bay production to date. Even though many of his films have strongly developed protagonists, and often feature fleshed-out supporting characters, *Pain & Gain* is the first time any character is given internal monologue voiceovers, let alone the fact that several players let us inside their heads throughout the film. Voice and point of view are key here. With Lugo, it makes us not only understand his motivations, but someone complicit in them. His desire to just chase the American Dream is likely to stir the passions of some audience members. A notable quote has him saying, "If you're willing to do the work, you can have anything. That's what makes the U.S. of A great. When it started, America was just a handful of scrawny colonies. Now, it's the most buff, pumped-up country on the planet.

That's pretty rad." The patriotism theme is further underlined when he says, "I have no sympathy for people who squander their gifts. It's sickening. It's worse than sickening. It's unpatriotic." By contrast, the internal monologue of Sorinia the stripper shows her to be completely naïve and perhaps a bit of a gold-digger.

As a script reader, I often had reason to equate voiceover with imperfect writing. Weak writers used the narration to express ideas they could have better communicated visually. It was a cheap short-cut and a crutch. That's not how it's deployed here, where confronting the audience with several distinct voices is done not only to perhaps raise awareness of the subjectivity of this adaptation of a real-life story, but also to trigger the identification with and alienation from other characters. There's also a nice irony in that we're confronted with a largely shallow cast of characters, yet their own voiceover reveals vast amounts of self-delusion regarding the depth of their desires. Lugo and Sorinia don't see themselves as vapid or superficial, and even while underlining their own entitlement, they remain oblivious to it. One key thing to take from their speeches is the total lack of self-awareness each of them has. No one should be able to look at this film and say that Michael Bay doesn't make films with sharp characters.

Sorinia might be mistaken to be the "Michael Bay woman" the director is often accused of exploiting. She's certainly beautiful and given the less-than-empowering occupation of "stripper." The character has little agency of her own and it's shown that she easily swallows Lugo's obvious lies because she's desperate to be with rich and powerful men. She's not exactly a role model for the women in the audience, but that seems to be by design. In fact, though she's not a participant in any of the schemes, the film makes a point of using her as a sign of moral corruption. Lugo acquires her first, and while it's vague enough that viewers who want to believe the best in Lugo might delude themselves into thinking he loves her, that's tossed out the window midway through the film.

Once the Kershaw theft is pulled off, Sorinia is passed from Lugo to Doyle like a trophy. And that's essentially what she is: a very pretty object and status symbol. Lugo doesn't care about her as a person at all and the discovery that she has no hard feelings either only underlines the business transaction that's occurring here. Furthermore, since Doyle is with her at that point, the affair highlights his own continuing moral corruption.

The film's other major female character is a total contrast. Like Sorinia, nurse Robin Peck (played by Rebel Wilson) is a blonde, but that's where the similarities stop. Sorinia has the body of a supermodel stripper, while Robin is a chubby plus-sized type. She also proves to be the moral center of the film. Sorinia doesn't even care to ask questions about what her lovers are into, and even up to the trial, she swallows their ridiculous lie. Robin displays a no-bullshit attitude that the other female lead lacks, but takes that even further when she divorces her husband prior to his trial specifically so she can testify against him. She's a crucial witness in bringing the gang down, yet another example of a strong female character in a Michael Bay film. The trial scene leaves little illusion about which character we're supposed to dismiss and which one we're supposed to cheer. In casting Robin against the presumed "Michael Bay women" type, perhaps it's the director's way of charting a new course, or at least alerting the audience not to expect the same familiar routines from him.

Further revelations might come not just from the subjects he chose to adapt from real life, but those elements he altered for the sake of the movie. By and large, the representations of Lugo and Doorbal are close to their real life incarnations, to the point of even retaining the same names. Kidnap victim Schiller is renamed and apparently give sleazier qualities than he had in real life, but the most notable departure may be the character of Paul Doyle, played by Dwayne "The Rock" Johnson. He's a composite based on three members of the gang. This script change could be motivated by a desire to keep the cast of characters manageable, but my own supposition is that this was also done to accommodate some of the themes Michael Bay wanted to use this story to express.

Paul Doyle may be an invention, but as played by The Rock, he is also a clear stand-in for Michael Bay. This should be an especially easy interpretation for Bay's critics to accept, as their narrative often paints Bay as an egotistical jerk. Who else would such an egomaniac cast as themselves but The Rock? (The fact the actor shares his name with one of Bay's early successes is a fortunate coincidence.)

In the film, Paul Doyle is an ex-con who initially has no interest in getting back into any illegal activity. Upon his release, he converts to Christianity and makes an honest go at being clean until his priest comes onto him, provoking a violent episode. Johnson's performance is often earnest, perhaps even to the point of seeming naïve. It would be a stretch to call him an innocent, but he's definitely corrupted by his company and is far from being the mastermind of the group. Before long, he's pulled into Lugo's plan of kidnapping and extortion, while believing that no one will get hurt in this scheme. He's promised that they'll all get rich and the reforming ex-con surely believes this will happen without consequence.

It's probably too simplistic and on the nose to attempt to read Lugo and Doorbal as direct stand-ins for Bay's original producers Jerry Bruckheimer and Don Simpson. They likely aren't represented by those characters as directly as Bay is by Doyle. At the very least, they represent the dark side of Hollywood. Bay escaped one form of imprisonment – making music videos – and was offered a chance to make a lot of money in feature films. His first five features were for a company built by two men who were known for making "harmless fun." So Bay joined them, but found the work to be spiritually empty. Unlike Doyle, he soon learned how to exert influence over his projects. Doyle never rises above being the second banana of the group.

Not only is Doyle easily picked out as the weak link by his captive, but he remains the one least comfortable with the grim tasks ahead of them when it becomes clear that Kershaw will have to be eliminated. In a moment so small it's easy to miss, we understand just how out of place Doyle is in this environment. Lugo, Doorbal and Doyle have staged a car accident and set Kershaw's car on fire. As the trio walks away in slow motion, the car explodes. At first, this appears to be just another execution of the "cool guy doesn't look at the explosion just ten feet behind him." Watch Doyle in this scene. When the explosion happens, he flinches. The other two guys keep moving like they're in an action film, but Doyle isn't truly one of them. He still has enough sense to feel the weight of what he does.

Think about everything we have discussed with Bay's earlier films. Big ideas have been present in his work from the beginning, albeit buried below the surface of the action movie clichés. Those sermons are so subtle that the action movie producers (the Lugos and Doorbals who initiated the scheme and brought Doyle on as a hired gun) don't even know to look for them. Lugo doesn't blink at a car explosion because he's fully accepted the role he plays.

One could see this movie as a dark comedy about despicable people. It certainly does what it can to prevent much sympathy for Kershaw. While the audience might abstractly recognize that murdering Kershaw would be wrong, at no point are they allowed to emotionally identify with him. For a while, it's played as if our sympathetic character will be Lugo, the guy who's just chasing the American Dream in his own screwed-up way. As the scheme progresses, Lugo reveals himself to be more and more corrupted, at which point the savvy audience members realize they're rooting for the wrong guy.

Paul Doyle is the real hero of this story, the story of his epic fall from grace and his eventual redemption. After the extortion and theft makes all three men rich, Paul gives in to his demons. He tosses religion aside, takes Lugo's girlfriend as his own, and indulges his drug habit. We see how he's totally seduced by the criminal lifestyle. His lowest moral point comes soon after, as he spirals into his addiction and shallow relationship. Depending on one's interpretation of *Bad Boys II*, this might be a metaphor for Bay losing himself in the visual excess of that earlier film, which was crippled by its spiritual emptiness.

Paul burns through his money, which forces him to do another job on his own. This parallels Bay spending all of his artistic capital on either *Pearl Harbor* or *The Island.* (Likely the latter, for while he was creatively attacked on *Pearl Harbor*, the film survived financially.) Thus, Paul falls back on the only thing he knows – crime. He pulls a robbery without his crew, akin to Bay making a film without Jerry Bruckheimer. It's a more brute robbery where not only does a dye pack blow up in his face but his toe gets shot off during his retreat. The metaphor might be more pointed if Doyle/Bay shot himself in the foot, but it could just as easily read as Hollywood hobbling him too.

Wounded and out of money, Doyle turns to his old collaborators who eagerly exploit his desperation to get him on board with their second extortion plan. We might even call this second plan "a sequel," you know, like *Transformers: Revenge of the Fallen* was. This scheme goes far worse than the first, as their attempt to scam Frank Griga and his wife fails when Griga isn't convinced. Worse, bumbling and rash action from Lugo results in Griga being grotesquely killed. (This too is a slight departure from real life, where it was Doorbal who killed Griga.) The analogy could well be Bay implicating his creative partners for everything that went wrong with the *Transformers* sequel.

A fascinating wrinkle is that Bay employs a toned-down version of his usual style. Though he indulges in a couple "hero rising into frame as camera spins" moments, this film might be his slowest-paced yet in terms of the average length between cuts. He also employs slow-motion more liberally than normal, particularly the ultra-slow-motion that kicks off the film during the police pursuit of Lugo. He seems to be training us to pace ourselves and take in the full breadth of what he's doing here.

It's notable that Doyle doesn't participate in the killings of either Griga or his wife, even though he's tasked with the gruesome clean-up. The business corrupted Doyle and at a point when his better judgment probably was telling him to walk away, he dove in deeper and found himself in a bigger mess. The connection to Bay himself couldn't be more obvious if it was skywritten. If you've seen the film, you probably remember what Paul Doyle does once the truth has been laid bare and the authorities have them in custody.

Doyle confesses.

He cleanses himself of his sins, rolls over on his co-conspirators. In doing so, not only does he avoid the death sentence the other two get, but he serves less than half of his 15-year sentence. Once out, he tries to make amends and reaffirms his Christian faith. We are seeing the beginning of Paul Doyle's redemption, but more importantly, this entire film is Michael Bay's confession, delivered only as Bay could do so.

With *Pain & Gain*, Bay throws himself on the mercy of his audience and through that disclosure, seeks to put all his past deeds behind him and clear the way for a new future. This film itself is a part of that future. Going forward from this point, we can and should expect to enjoy a new era in Bay's filmmaking. We have already discussed how his subsequent film *Transformers: Age of Extinction* is in many ways a subversion of every value that series once represented. The earlier *Transformers* films were responsible for pushing Bay to his spiritual awakening, with *Pain & Gain* being the outlet for that catharsis and *Age of Extinction* showing us Michael Bay revisiting that world with his eyes open. It is an epilogue to the darker period of his filmmaking career. Taken with *Pain & Gain*, *Transformers: Age of Extinction* redeems the journey to get there.

The transformation Bay experienced through those series of projects means whatever comes next will be the beginning of the next phase of his career, as distinct from the previous phases as his post-Bruckheimer projects were from his first five films. Art can tell us as much about the artist as it does the message the artist is trying to convey. Just because a director fails to bluntly wear their heart on their sleeves in the manner of a Taylor Swift breakup song, it doesn't mean that their work isn't deeply personal. *Pain & Gain* makes that identification harder to overlook and in turn, should prompt reexamination of the film's Bay made to get him to the point of making a confession.

Pain & Gain is a cry for help. Let us hope that history shows it did not go unheeded.

Final Thoughts

The Michael Bay filmography is not the story of explosions and killer robots. It is the epic saga of one visionary's artistic maturation. Most great artists go unappreciated in their time, so the critical drubbing Bay experiences regularly might not be an anomaly. But hopefully this book has helped you appreciate how this director is a keen observer of the human condition, and how some of the most successful films of all time can contain some of the most political and spiritual themes of this era of filmmaking.

As I worked on this tome, it was my intention to keep the project incredibly secret until it was ready for release. The deeper I got into the writing, the more eager I was to tell people what I had been working on. In a way, I was also inspired to do so after reading a number of accounts about how often Michael Bay cited his target audience as his motivation for a particular element of his movies.

Love him or hate him, you can't say that Bay doesn't have "audience satisfaction" at the top of his priorities. As we discussed in the chapters on *The Rock* and *Armageddon*, more than once he went to bat for sequences and elements that his collaborators (and really, his bosses) didn't think were necessary. And yet, Bay was right. He knows what his target audience wants and he's able to deliver it to the masses. His own commercial success speaks for itself. Success doesn't mean "having zero detractors." You don't need me to tell you that plenty of critics and moviegoers make regular sport of attacking the man. Yet he's gotten the last laugh because he's put in the effort to entertain such a large majority that the detractors are insignificant.

"Audience satisfaction" led me to tell some trusted friends about my project, largely to allow me to gauge their reactions. The vast majority were immediately positive, and this was a crowd made up of people who both loved and hated the director. Several of them asked me a question that I probably should have expected.

"What's the next book? You should do Brett Ratner!" (McG was a popular alternative as well.)

Giving an answer to this question and suggestion inadvertently led me to exploring why I began this book in the first place. The only things that Ratner and McG have in common with Bay is that all three tend to be critical punching bags and they often work in action films. Each are successful in their own right, but Bay is on a completely different plane. As we discussed in the Introduction, Bay's commercial success puts him on a par with some of the most acclaimed and successful directors of our time. He's unlocked the same crowd-pleasing formulas as Spielberg and Cameron, but without earning a great deal of respect along the way.

That's what made examining his films in depth such a fascinating prospect. If they're so "bad," then what keeps people from coming back time and time again? What is the secret sauce that separates him from the Brett Ratners of the industry? The prospect of examining Ratner's filmography one film at a time is less enticing because his track record doesn't have such a large disconnect from critical opinion that one is left wondering if the man has been unfairly maligned.

True, just because McDonald's is the most ubiquitous and most successful restaurant in the free world doesn't mean it's necessarily the greatest. But it *does* mean that they are doing something consistently right and filling a need better than any of their competitors. Calling McDonald's food "garbage" would be so easy. Isn't it more interesting to explore their product and method and understand what puts them so far ahead of Jack in the Box?

For now, I choose to consider that the lesson of Michael Bay's work is that we need not sacrifice the biblical for bombast, nor must we choose between the visceral and the virtuous. His best films teach us that emotional resonance and explosion can go hand in hand, while even his rare misfires show us that even a flawed film is far more compelling when it's striving to say something.

Taking such a close look at Michael Bay's films left me with a genuinely new appreciation for what he's accomplished. I hoped to write a book that could be enjoyed by Michael Bay's biggest fans and his harshest critics alike. If you disagree with me, that's fine. I only hope that you enjoyed the conversation. After all, isn't it more satisfying to contemplate that his work truly his more than hot women and hotter explosions? And if it really was that easy, wouldn't everyone do it? I began this book convinced that there had to be more to a Michael Bay movie than that. I hope exploring those possibilities was as fun for you to read as it was for me to write.

Michael Bay filmography

<u>As a director</u>
Bad Boys (1995)
The Rock (1996)
Armageddon (1998)
Pearl Harbor (2001)
Bad Boys II (2003)
The Island (2005)
Transformers (2007)
Transformers: Revenge of the Fallen (2009)
Transformers: Dark of the Moon (2011)
Pain & Gain (2013)
Transformers: Age of Extinction (2014)

<u>As a producer</u>
Armageddon (1998)
Pearl Harbor (2001)
The Texas Chainsaw Massacre (2003)
The Amityville Horror (2005)
The Island (2005)
The Texas Chainsaw Massacre: The Beginning (2006)
The Hitcher (2007)
Transformers (2007)
The Unborn (2009)
Friday the 13th (2009)
Horsemen (2009)
Transformers: Revenge of the Fallen (2009)
A Nightmare on Elm Street (2010)
I Am Number Four (2011)
Transformers: Dark of the Moon (2011)
Pain & Gain (2013)
The Purge (2013)
The Purge: Anarchy (2014)
Teenage Mutant Ninja Turtles (2014)
Ouija (2014)
Project Almanac (2015)

Music Videos, as a director
"Soldier of Love" (1989) – Donny Osmond
"Angelia" (1989) – Richard Marx
"I'll Be Holding On" (1989) – Greg Allman
"I'll Love You" (1991) – Vanilla Ice
"I Touch Myself" (1991) – The Divinyls
"Love Thing" (1992) – Tina Turner
"Do It To Me" (1992) – Lionel Richie
"You Won't See Me Cry" (1992) – Wilson Phillips
"I'd Do Anything for Love (But I Won't Do That)" (1993) – Meat Loaf
"Rock and Roll Dreams Come Through" (1994) – Meat Loaf
"Objects in the Rear View Mirror May Appear Closer Than They Are" (1994) – Meat Loaf
"Falling in Love (Is Hard on the Knees)" (1997) – Aerosmith
"There You'll Be" (2001) – Faith Hill.

Acknowledgements

None of my career in Hollywood, nor likely anything else I have achieved in life, would have been possible without the love and support of my parents, particularly when I moved across the country and depended on their generosity to pay my rent every month for a while. And believe me, my family's far from rich, so this was hardly no big deal for them.

I also must acknowledge the love and support of my beautiful wife. When you find the right girl (or guy) marry them, kids. Best choice you can ever make.

Many thanks to my friend Kat Abbott, who copy-edited an early version of this book and caught a lot my sloppy errors. The post-revision errors are all on me, but she did her best to eliminate my gaffes.

The absolutely gorgeous cover you hold in your hands was the work of Keith Richner. It far exceeded my hopes and I will be getting a blow-up to hang on my wall.

To all my English teachers throughout school, thanks for seeing I had a talent for writing and encouraging it.

To my film professors, thank you for giving me the tools to make the case for Michael Bay. I'm sure you're proud.

And this acknowledgment page would not be complete without paying tribute to the man who's the reason we're all here. Michael - thanks for some really fun movies.

About the Author

The Bitter Script Reader started reading scripts professionally in Hollywood in 2003. After a few years working in development, he became an agency script reader at one of the largest and most successful agencies in the business.

Having seen just about every imaginable way a script could go wrong, the Bitter Script Reader shares what he's learned on his blog at http://thebitterscriptreader.blogspot.com. The site has been in operation since 2009 and offers writers the insight of someone who's read enough scripts to know the wrong way to write. His perspective is representative of the gatekeepers that a young writer's script will need to get past in order to build a career.

The Bitter Script Reader has written columns for the websites *Film School Rejects* and *KsiteTV* and is on Twitter at @BittrScrptReadr. He also can be found dispensing screenwriting advice through a puppet on his YouTube channel and can be reached via email at zuulthereader@gmail.com.

Source Notes

Introduction

Box Office Mojo, People Index, Directors, By Gross. http://boxofficemojo.com/people/?view=Director&sort=sumgross&order=DESC&p=.htm

Hoffman, Lori. "Broken 'Transformers.'" *Atlantic City Weekly*, July 2, 2014. http://www.atlanticcityweekly.com/arts-and-entertainment/movie-reviews/Broken__Transformers_-265597441.html

Jones, Alan. "Transformers: Age of Extinction." *RadioTimes*. http://www.radiotimes.com/film/cnpj8k/transformers-age-of-extinction

Miller, Neil. "The Summer Movie Diaries: Biggest, Loudest, Teeth Like a Dinobot." *Film School Rejects*. July 8, 2014. http://filmschoolrejects.com/features/summer-movies-transformers-x-men-300.php

Chapter 1: Transformers: Age of Extinction (2014)

Ebert, Roger. "Arlington Road." *The Chicago Sun-Times*, July 9, 1999. http://www.rogerebert.com/reviews/arlington-road-1999

Shotz, Dan. "Alum Finds Hollywood Film Fame." *The Wesleyan Argus*, February 5, 1999. Archived at: http://michaelbay.com/articles/alum-find-hollywood-fame/

Chapter 2: Bad Boys (1995)

Boucher, Geoff. "Michael Bay Knows You Hate Him: 'There's a lot of poison on the Internet… whatever." *The Los Angeles Times*, May 22, 2009. http://herocomplex.latimes.com/uncategorized/michael-bay-blows-it-up-real-good-140-terrabytes-used-for-transformers-2-effects/

Gleiberman, Owen. "Bad Boys." *Entertainment Weekly*, April 21, 1995. http://www.ew.com/ew/article/0,,296885,00.html

Fennessey, Sean. "Blow-Up: An Oral History of Michael Bay, the Most Explosive Director of All Time." *GQ Magazine*, July 2011. http://www.gq.com/entertainment/movies-and-tv/201107/michael-bay-oral-history

Wolf, Craig. "In The Dressing Room with Dana Carvey; Every Night Live?" *The New York Times*, December 21, 1992. http://www.nytimes.com/1992/12/31/garden/in-the-dressing-room-with-dana-carvey-every-night-live.html

Chapter 3: The Rock (1996)

Bay, Michael. Director's commentary, *The Rock* blu-ray.

Cohen, David S. "Michael Bay, Seriously." *Daily Variety*, June 28, 2011. http://variety.com/2011/film/features/michael-bay-seriously-1118039082/

Ebert, Roger. "The Rock." *The Chicago Sun-Times*, June 7, 1996. http://www.rogerebert.com/reviews/the-rock-1996

Internet Movie Database, "The Rock (1996) – Trivia" http://www.imdb.com/title/tt0117500/trivia

Welkos, Robert. "'Cable,' 'Rock' in Disputes on Writing Credits. *The Los Angeles Times*, May 21, 1996. http://articles.latimes.com/1996-05-21/entertainment/ca-6461_1_screen-credit

Chapter 4: Armageddon (1998)

Affleck, Ben. Commentary, Armageddon: The Criterion Collection blu-ray.

Bay, Michael. Commentary, Armageddon: The Criterion Collection blu-ray.

Basinger, Jeanine. "Armageddon." Armageddon: The Criterion Collection blu-ray. Archived at: http://www.criterion.com/current/posts/48-armageddon

Dean, Jeremy. "13 Miliseconds: The Incredible Speed at Which Your Brain Can Identify an Image." Psyblog, January 22, 2014. http://www.spring.org.uk/2014/01/13-milliseconds-the-incredible-speed-at-which-your-brain-can-identify-an-image.php

Ebert, Roger. "Armageddon." *The Chicago Sun-Times*, July 1, 1998. http://www.rogerebert.com/reviews/armageddon-1998

Internet Movie Database, "Armageddon (1998) – Trivia" http://www.imdb.com/title/tt0120591/trivia

MichaelBay.com. Armageddon Production Notes. http://michaelbay.com/media/articles/010/010.html

Chapter 5: Pearl Harbor (2001)

Bay, Michael. Commentary, Armageddon: The Criterion Collection blu-ray.

Ebert, Roger. "Pearl Harbor." The Chicago Sun-Times, May 25, 2001. http://www.rogerebert.com/reviews/pearl-harbor-2001

Fennessey, Sean. "Blow-Up: An Oral History of Michael Bay, the Most Explosive Director of All Time." *GQ Magazine*, July 2011. http://www.gq.com/entertainment/movies-and-tv/201107/michael-bay-oral-history

Sunshine, Linda. *Pearl Harbor: The Movie and the Moment*. Hyperion, 2001.

Chapter 7: The Island (2005)

Blackfilm Staff. "The Island: An Interview with Scarlett Johansson and Michael Bay." Blackfilm.com, July 2005. http://www.blackfilm.com/20050715/features/theislandinterviews.shtml

Carroll, Larry. "Michael Bay Finding Himself Stranded With 'Island.'" *MTV News*, July 21, 2005. http://www.mtv.com/news/1506139/michael-bay-finding-himself-stranded-with-island/

Ebert, Roger. "The Island." *The Chicago Sun-Times*, July 21, 2005. http://www.rogerebert.com/reviews/the-island-2005

Playlist Staff, "Retrospective: The Films of Michael Bay." *The Playlist*, June 23, 2014.

http://blogs.indiewire.com/theplaylist/retropective-the-films-of-michael-bay-20140623

Ryan, Mike. "Michael Bay, 'Transformers 4' Director, On The Struggles of 'Pain & Gain.'" *The Huffington Post*, September 21, 2012. http://www.huffingtonpost.com/2012/09/21/michael-bay-transformers-4-pain-and-gain_n_1903523.html

Chapter 8: Transformers (2007)

Ebert, Roger. "Transformers." *The Chicago Sun-Times*, July 5, 2007. http://www.rogerebert.com/reviews/transformers-2007

Fennessey, Sean. "Blow-Up: An Oral History of Michael Bay, the Most Explosive Director of All Time." *GQ Magazine*, July 2011. http://www.gq.com/entertainment/movies-and-tv/201107/michael-bay-oral-history

Itzkoff, Dave. "Character-Driven Films (but Keep the Kaboom.) *The New York Times*, June 24, 2007. http://www.nytimes.com/2007/06/24/movies/24dave.html?pagewanted=1&_r=0

Chapter 9: Transformers: Revenge of the Fallen (2009)

Billington, Alex. "Kicking Off 2009 with Writers Alex Kurtzman and Roberto Orci – Part Two: Transformers 2." *FirstShowing.net*, January 14, 2009. http://www.firstshowing.net/2009/kicking-off-2009-with-writers-alex-kurtzman-and-roberto-orci-part-two-transformers-2/

Ebert, Roger. "Transformers: Revenge of the Fallen." *The Chicago Sun-Times*, June 23, 2009. http://www.rogerebert.com/reviews/transformers-revenge-of-the-fallen-2009

Fernandez, Jay A. "Heavy metal for sequel." *The Los Angeles Times*, October 10, 2007. http://articles.latimes.com/2007/oct/10/entertainment/et-scriptland10

Travers, Peter. "Transformers: Revenge of the Fallen." *Rolling Stone*, June 24, 2009. http://www.rollingstone.com/movies/reviews/transformers-revenge-of-the-fallen-20090624

Wilonsky, Robert. "Michael Bay Can't Live Up to Michael Bay in Transformers Part 2." *The Village Voice*, June 24, 2009. http://www.villagevoice.com/2009-06-24/film/michael-bay-can-t-live-up-to-michael-bay-in-transformers-part-2/

Chapter 11: Pain & Gain (2013)

Alvarado, Francisco. "Pain & Gain: Where the Real-Life Sung Gym Gang Characters Are Now." *The Miami New Times*, April 4, 2013. http://www.miaminewtimes.com/2013-04-04/news/pain-and-gain-where-the-real-life-sun-gym-gang-characters-are-now/full/

Bamberger, Michael. *The Man Who Heard Voices; Or, How M. Night Shyamalan Risked His Life on a Fairy Tale.* Gotham. 2006

Bay, Michael. "Michael Bay Talks Transformers 4, Pain & Gain." MichaelBay.com, February 13, 2012.

http://michaelbay.com/blog/files/e9660a11c44f8c2fb00b2b9cc19ed822-750.php

Bay, Michael. "Pain and Gain info/Hollywood Reporter correction." MichaelBay.com, March 6, 2012. http://www.michaelbay.com/blog/files/87c4ab1ca60ec4850c45bf6c52af599b-754.php

Vary, Adam B. "Optimus Prime Time." *Entertainment Weekly*, July 5, 2007.
http://www.ew.com/ew/article/0,,20044598,00.html

Printed in Great Britain
by Amazon.co.uk, Ltd.,
Marston Gate.